Animations

For Your Layout

*Easy Techniques to Bring
Your Layout to Life!*

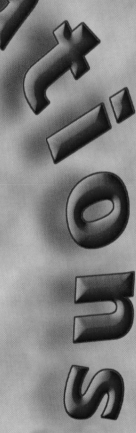

by Roy Everett

*with Photos by
Fred M. Dole*

Cover Design by Jeff LaBarre
Cover Photographs by Fred M. Dole
Book Design by Fred M. Dole

Published by the Myron J. Biggar Group, Inc.
PO Box 239
65 S Broad St.
Nazareth PA 18064-0239
Phone 610-759-0406
Fax 610-759-0223
E-Mail OGaugeRwy@aol.com

ISBN 0-9650291-4-X
Printed in the United States of America

Contents

About the Author

Roy (Seth L.) Everett was born in Pittsburgh, PA on March 18, 1936, the "high water-mark" day of the greatest flood, which the city has ever seen! His first train set (Lionel Set No. 845W), received in December 1941, was the beginning of the Little Lakes Lines (LLL).

In the Whitehall/Baldwin Township area of Pittsburgh, PA, Roy began to actively create and fabricate animated scenes for the LLL from 1950 through 1953. Animated scenes were developed for placement each year on a series of 10' x 25' living room floor layouts. Here track was laid on white bed sheets for snow scenes, which were later dyed brown to imitate summer scenery. Layout configuration and the accompanying animated scenes were completely changed with significant upgrades each year. Each layout was operational from mid-November through mid-March. A "permanent" open frame wood, screen, and plaster layout was constructed and operated from fall 1953 through spring 1958. The "Toonerville Traction Company" and "Podunk & Mousebelly" branch line came into being on this layout, as did the LLL's Buena Vista Amusement Park.

Upon graduating from the Carnegie Institute of Technology, Pittsburgh, PA as an electrical engineer, Roy moved to New Jersey and worked for the U.S. Army Research & Development Laboratories at Fort Monmouth. There, in the course of 35 years, he has obtained 10 United States and 2 Canadian patents in the area of electrical/mechanical/optical devices. He married Elaine King in November 1963, and they have two sons, Glenn and Gregg. (Both have trains around their trees at Christmas.)

The present LLL layout was begun in 1974 and has been gradually expanding since. Many of the original animations constructed in the 1950's are still in operation today, almost half a century later. Dozens of new animations on the current layout have become increasingly sophisticated. These are now electronically controlled and feature complete scenes, which often provide multiple animation effects.

Roy, now retired from the electronic engineering profession, is pursuing an alternate career in freelance writing. Other interests include volunteering on the Pinelands Cultural Society (PCS) Executive Board, where he served as president for three years during which the full-sized 6,000 square foot Albert Music Hall was designed and built. (A downsized animated model of the original Hall is presented in the "Country Animations" section.) Roy also serves as design editor and desktop publisher of the PCS newsletter. Travel and continued improvement of the Little Lakes Lines round out his current plans.

Introduction

Life is fascinating. Our senses are tuned to continual stimulation by the sights and sounds about us. Train layouts inherently emulate a slice of life. An engine running on a single loop of track has this quality. It moves. It makes noise. The headlight beam sweeps about the room. It becomes "alive"... and yes, fascinating.

Train layouts become increasingly personal and alive as they expand. As more trains, track, and accessories are added, a miniature world begins to evolve. This world intentionally, or otherwise, tends to reflect the life experiences and personality of the builder. As the layout becomes more complex, the sights and sounds emanating from it multiply. The appeal of the entire display increases, as does the viewer's fascination with it. Perhaps this is an important reason why model railroad layouts are so appealing to most everyone from the youngest child to the eldest adult. It is a basic appeal which is not just limited to those who happen to enjoy the study and operation of the trains themselves.

The purpose of this book is to introduce a fresh way for you to think about your own layout. Look beyond thinking in terms of simply adding off-the-shelf store-bought items designed by someone else. Seek out those areas where custom animations may be logically used to increase your layout's appeal. Review your own life experiences and personal interests to help identify scene vignettes of uncommon interest to yourself. Animated scenes do require time and effort to construct. Such time would be best spent creating scenes of significant rather than just passing personal interest. Your reward for following such a path is that you will have created something with a deeper personal meaning. While friends and visitors will enjoy and be entertained by your efforts, the greatest pleasure will be your own.

The subject is introduced via a brief tour of my own layout, the Little Lakes Lines (LLL). My thinking process upon which the LLL has evolved is outlined. This process is most important. In order to achieve something, it is imperative that you first decide and then plan just what is to be accomplished. Through example, the ways in which animated scenes were created, fabricated and then incorporated on the LLL layout are shown. Each of the animations has one or more of what I call the five basic "Animation Elements". These are (1) Light, (2) Motion, (3) Sound, (4) Smoke, and (5) Time. Each by itself is quite ordinary. It is through the judicious combining of these elements, that truly outstanding animated scenes can be realized.

Animated scenes may be controlled by elementary electrical/electronic circuitry. Chapter 2 defines the electrical terms and symbols used in this book. Six basic animation control circuits are described in Chapter 3. Each consists of just four to nine common components. They are not difficult to build nor do they require any critical adjustment for their operation. These circuits, used independently or in combination, can bring most any animated scene to life!

Detailed examples of over 20 animated scenes from the LLL's layout are presented in Chapters 4 through 7. They have been grouped into four broad categories: Amusement Park, City, Country and Railroad Yard. The ideas are many and varied. These scenes may be directly duplicated or extensively modified for use on your own layout. Although they range from the simple to fairly complex, it will become evident in the following pages that one need not be a rocket scientist, computer guru, or master model builder in order to build effective and interesting animated scenes. There are certainly many ways to accomplish the same thing.

Information on material sources and a bibliography is also included.

So... read on! Hopefully, the thoughts and creations presented in this book will not just entertain, but will in some way contribute to adding new interest to your layout!

- Roy Everett

Chapter One

The Little Lakes Lines Animated Layout

My Little Lakes Lines (LLL) is a three rail, semi-scale layout, approximately 12' x 28' in size, which has an extensive number of electronically controlled animations. All are of original design and home-built. Over 1,700 miniature lights, 50 motors and 20 audio channels are used to bring the many scenes to life. Well over 2,000 figures populate the layout (I am sure that they greatly enjoy the animated sights and sounds about them). Yes, there are trains too, but their motors and lights are not included in the previous numbers. I have built numerous layouts each featuring an extensive variety of animations since 1950. The layout discussed herein began in the fall of 1974.

Background

This particular version of the LLL did not just happen. My basic premise was to create a layout, which would have a purpose from a railroad point-of-view and also contain a variety of animated scenes. I wanted to not only model specific scenes which I had found interesting over the years, but also to convey the ambiance and feeling of these places and things. The layout is designed to generally reflect the topography of the Pittsburgh, PA area where I spent the first 22 years of my life. I lived in the Whitehall section of Baldwin Township, about 6 miles south of Pittsburgh, up through the late 1950's.

Pittsburgh terrain is characterized by steep hills with streams (often called "runs") and rivers flanked by heavy industry winding through narrow valleys. Consequently, there are a multitude of bridges and tunnels used by both automobile roads and the rail lines. The Pittsburgh region is most interesting from a railroad point-of-view. In the 1950's, the city was very closely tied together via multiple trolley lines, along with passenger, heavy freight and industrial railroads. I had many occasions to ride the various trolley lines, main line Pennsylvania trains and to visit heavy industry (e.g. Jones & Laughton Steel, Mesta Machine, Fisher Body) which utilized industrial railroad equipment.

The LLL is chronologically set in the early 1960's. Steam is the predominate motive power for the railroad. Coal is plentiful and steam locomotive servicing facilities are deeply entrenched in the LLL's area as they were in the Pittsburgh region. A few early diesel types do infrequently traverse the rails. Fairbanks-Morse Trainmasters and GM F-3's are about as modern as it gets! The LLL model railroad emulates Pittsburgh's true-life arrangement of allowing one to travel by Class I rail, then transfer to trolleys within the city or out to neighboring towns and points of interest via various interurban lines. Pittsburgh on the LLL is represented by Podunk City. Pittsburgh's city trolley system becomes the Podunk

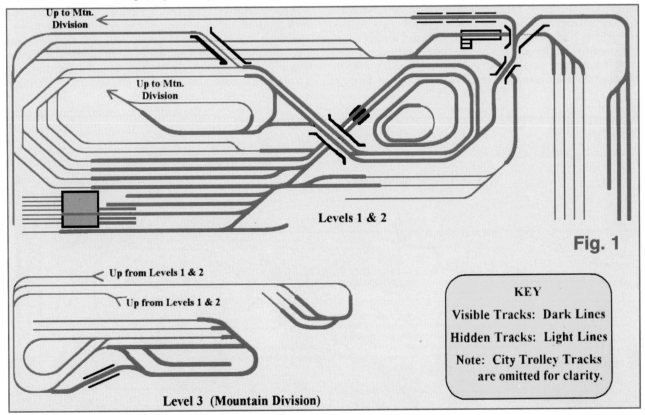

Left: Great piles of junk fill Chet's Scrap yard. Pieces of old toy train transformer laminations, dumped by the fence, make excellent material for the magnetic crane to load into waiting gondolas. The operating coaling tower (center-rear) uses a well-disguised Lionel No. 97 Coal Elevator mechanism. Plastic tea leaf sprigs provide the lush vegetation sprouting about the heaps of junk.

Traction Co. and the interurban line is the Toonerville Traction Company. Pittsburgh's trolleys connect to the still-operating Kennywood Amusement Park, whereas the Toonerville Traction Company connects to the Buena Vista Amusement Park. Both the real and the model amusement parks are perched high on hills overlooking a river and rail lines below.

Figure 1 shows the overall LLL track layout. Hidden trackage is used in the front as well as towards the rear of the layout to give the viewer the impression that the trains are really traveling to a distant location. I consider the trains themselves as animations, which change, often unexpectedly, with the greatest practical variety due to the placement of concealed tracks, cuts, multiple levels and mountains. Each train travels through a scenic area once and then goes elsewhere for a considerably longer amount of time. Any given train may also be followed by a completely different one. This operational effect is accomplished by the track layout, which provides for extensive interconnection of rail lines with numerous hidden staging yards. I use different embodiments of this concept for each of the automated trolley lines.

The Little Lakes Lines Scenic Theme Partitioning

Scenic theme partitioning is useful in that it allows one to focus in a particular definitive direction to develop structures, sight and sound animations unique to and in support of the main idea. (i.e. Free-lance modeling of trains and trolleys in a Pittsburgh-like locale.) I have taken specific steps to develop four explicit scenic theme areas on my layout. These are (1) City, (2) Train Yard, (3) Country-River & Mountains and (4) Amuse-ment Park. You may notice that these scenic theme areas are not particularly remarkable. They are indeed, very general partitions. However, the intent here is to first broadly categorize the major scenes and then proceed to do everything possible to insure each one has and retains it's own unique identity. This method of thinking has added immense pleasure to me as the builder. I also believe that visitors receive heightened enjoyment when

viewing the layout where animated sights and sounds of the model scenes make logical real world sense. The relative spatial relationships between the four major scenic theme regions on the Little Lakes Lines are shown in Figure 2. As real estate is always at a premium on model layouts, steep mountains, low valley areas, thick foliage, and deep cuts are used to force visual and audible separation of the scenic theme regions.

As one moves about the layout's edge, different scenic theme areas come within view. It gives the impression that an entirely different layout is being viewed from each subsequent vantage point. For example, when observing the hustle and bustle of Podunk City, the train yard and platforms can be seen down below the city. Far in the distance, a glimpse of the Buena Vista Amusement Park lights peeking above a grove of trees perched high on the top of Bumpy Top Mountain can be seen. Major country scenes cannot be viewed at all from the city. Mole Hill Mine, the neighboring coke ovens and the tranquil Rocky River area are completely hidden on the far side of the mountain ridge.

A closer pictorial look at each of the LLL's Scenic Theme Areas will serve to illustrate the thinking I used to create the various scenic vignettes and the many personalized animations associated with each. Perhaps some thought-provoking ideas will surface for adapting these or other animations for your own layout.

Scenic Theme Area #1: The City (Podunk City)

My goal for the large city scenic theme area is to give the impression that this is a truly vibrant city with major stores, restaurants, a theatre, a town square park, passenger terminal, freight house, electrical generation station and a metropolitan trolley system with a five trolley car barn. This is a big order for a model railroad. You may think that it would require an enormous amount of space to create such a scene. Not so. Podunk City encompasses just 16 square feet on my layout, including space for the entire city trolley system. Further, the whole city is raised on a second level platform so that it

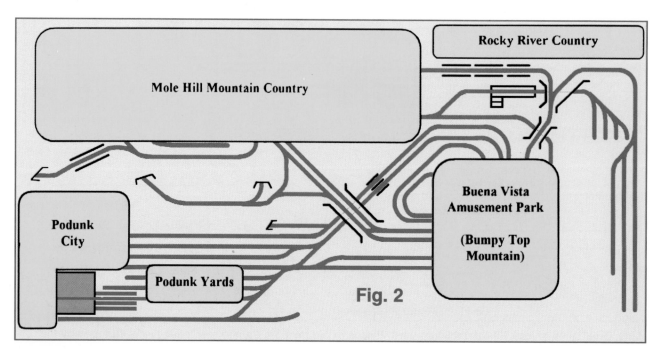

takes absolutely no space away from the main train layout's real estate.

The Little Lakes Lines terminal operationally connects Podunk City to the remainder of the layout. Passengers and freight enter through street level buildings. They then proceed via inside stairs or elevators to the trains at the platforms below. Arriv-ing persons exit the terminal at the street level. Here they may hail a taxi or walk a short block to catch a trolley. They may also pause at Whyte's Bite Shop for a burger or cross the street to Finn's Saloon for some entertainment and a liquid lunch. (Finn's serves the best sarsaparilla and Moxie drinks east of the Mississippi!)

Podunk City buildings employ a number of eye-fooling deceptions in order to appear larger than they are in reality. The base of the city is 3' from the floor with buildings rising to a height of almost 5' above floor level They are positioned high enough so that it is not quite so obvious that many are only 3" deep. All buildings have generous size windows with interior detailing and lighting. Small pocket mirrors are discretely positioned inside selected buildings at 45° angles to reveal detailed scenes of considerably greater depth than the actual 3" of the structure. Buildings also serve to mask the trolley's run as it goes out of eyesight down a street between them. This suggests that it is heading on to another section of the city, which makes Podunk seem larger than in actuality.

Cities offer interesting

Day and night at Podunk City. Building interiors spring to life after the sun goes down! Only select low level decorative bulbs may be directly viewed. Individual rooms are either directly lighted via concealed bulbs, lit through their doorways or left dark to add realism and interest. All rooms have interior details as even non-illumined areas receive some glow through their windows from the layout room's ambient light.

opportunities for animation. Every musician in the 20 piece city park band gazebo, as well as the conductor, independently move about as Sousa march music is played from a speaker concealed in the roof of the bandstand gazebo. Music from the H.M.S. Pinafore may be heard from the ornate Podunk Arts Center with its dazzling walking light marquee. Upstairs at the Podunk School of Dance, four aspiring ballet dancers may be seen individually practicing pirouettes. Some spinning slow, others quicker, with each occasionally pausing to rest. Roy's Hobby Shop has a model train complete with headlight and rear drumhead light, which endlessly travels through mountain scenery in the store's window. In the street outside Roy's window, a tow truck with flashing lights is unsuccessfully trying to help a man to get his balky car started. The car periodically makes a series of coughing sounds as clouds of smoke belch from its tail

pipe. Unfortunately, it is never quite able to run. A foot-stompin' ragtime music show is in session across the street in Finn's Saloon. The upbeat sound of bar room piano, banjo, and happy singing can be heard ringing out from the main entrance. Inside, a dancer is moving about in the spotlight on the small foot-lighted stage next to the mirrored bar. Finn's outside light-rimmed sign flashes bright and dim beckoning others to come in and join the fun! Mounted high on the Sears building is Podunk's famous smoking billboard. The man in the cigarette advertisement continuously blows out puffs of smoke, sometimes creating incredible rings! Randomly periodic train announcements emanate from the upper level of the Podunk City Station.

I also use the Podunk Traction Company trolleys as an animation element. There are two trolley cars on the single-track line. They emerge automatically from the car barn, run around two sides of the city park, randomly making all combination of stops at three different locations. They then travel out of sight down the city street between large buildings to the unseen sections of the city. The viewer may see none, one or both trolleys present at their stops around the city at any given time. The trolley's lights remain on, even when stopped for the traveler's convenience. The powerhouse directly behind the car barn contains dual generators, which produce the fictitious 25-cycle electricity to run the trolleys. The entire generating plant may be viewed through huge casement windows. When operating, each generator has an indicator lamp, which can be seen flickering at the 25-cycle rate.

Numerous sound effects help to bring Podunk City to life. Miscellaneous city traffic sounds operate continuously in the background. Specialized sounds, coupled with animations as previously discussed, originate from specific locations. Care has been taken to place the sound sources directly within the animated model structures by using miniature speakers. This ensures that the observer will associate the sound with the intended site. I also attempt to physically separate the specialized sounds from each other as much as practical so that they may be effectively heard when one is in close proximity of a specific model. Upon moving away from the scene, the sounds blend into a lively cacophony of "city-type" noise.

Scenic Theme Area #2:
Railroad Yard (Podunk Yards)

My objective for the train yard theme area was to create the feeling of a large, depressingly grimy, dirty facility capable of servicing and performing heavy repairs on large steam engines. It also had to be capable of storing a dozen or more locomotives. As with the city, layout real estate was at a premium. Space problems were exacerbated by the LLL's mandatory use of Lionel O gauge sectional track and turnouts. I concentrated upon designing a yard, which would satisfy my objectives, yet require minimal room. The answer was to construct a transfer table to shuttle locomotives between very closely spaced servicing/storage tracks rather than a conventional roundhouse and turntable which would require an enormous amount of room to house a like number of engines. (A wye located in the foothills of Mole Hill Mountain is used when locomotive turning is required.) Locating the heavy service shops beneath the city further reduced the dimensions of the yard. The final design required just 20 square feet on the visible layout. It includes servicing and storage for up to 20 locomotives, 8 bay locomotive maintenance facility, coal elevator, water tank, scrap yard with a magnetic crane, ice house, paint shop, sign shop, oil tanks, and even a hobo jungle.

The railroad yard animations are quite varied. The transfer table is the main attraction as it slowly moves locomotives between the 10 service stub tracks. When the table is in motion, the motor generator can be seen revolving in the control shed. A welding scene is located in the heavy repair shop with its erratic bright blue-white light casting dancing shadows around the adjacent machinery. Never-ending buckets of coal are hauled to the top hopper of the coal elevator. Adjacent to the coal elevator is the Seaboard Ice Company's icehouse. Shimmering blocks of ice creep along the upper platform by conveyor into position for stocking non-

Podunk Engine Yards: The 8-bay underground engine repa[ir] facility (left) is accessed via an automatic screw-drive[n] transfer table (above). A motor/generator set mechanis[m] made from an electric drill armature revolves in the orang[e] control house when the table is active.

mechanical reefers. I incorporated a hobo jungle scene at the base of a floodlight tower. This scene includes a group of hobos singing, playing guitars, and drinking sassafras tea. Tiny lanterns provide illumination as they gather around a burning barrel for warmth from the nighttime chill. The animated barrel has a flickering red glow. When visitors press a nearby button, smoke begins to flow from the barrel. It then crackles, pops, and erupts with puffs of smoke as one of the men must have just tossed a handful of popcorn into the fire! As the barrel quiets down, sounds of Woody Guthrie and Cisco Houston playing guitar and singing railroad-oriented songs really make this scene come alive!

Bumpy Top Mountain rises across the Rocky River gorge as seen from the roof of the Mole Hill Mine Company perched high in the Mole Hill Mountain range. The Mole Hill Mine, a rare shaft-type iron ore mine, and the three "beehive" coke ovens (near left) produce essential raw materials for steel production.

A track gang is now in the process of finishing their work by burning an accumulation of old railroad ties by the yard throat. The stack of ties is smoldering with bright red and yellow coals. Smoke periodically flows out of the pile with every shift of the wind. The LLL's Switch Tower T-1 stands at the very entrance to the yard. Observers can see the Centralized Traffic Control (CTC) panel inside the tower. The CTC diagram resembles that of the LLL's yard track layout and contains several miniature lights. These lights randomly change with time as the trainmen in the tower constantly work to assure that all turnouts are properly positioned.

There is a very complex multi-track road crossing by Tower T-1. Two standard cross bucks with alternating red lights, a single white light warning stand with bell, and a railroad employee with a sign all stand guard to protect this important crossing. The entire warning system is automatically activated when a train approaches and remains active for a period of time after it passes.

Scenic Theme Area #3: Country (Mole Hill Mountains & Rocky River)

Mountains perform multiple purposes on the Little Lakes Lines. I use them to conceal train staging areas, to preserve major scene partitions by blocking undesirable observer viewpoints, to provide interesting multi-level terrain for the railroad right-of-way and to serve as a general background for the overall display. Vegetation on the mountains varies from heavily wooded sections behind Podunk City to the almost barren red rock region by the Mole Hill Mining Company.

I have left most of the mountain area in a forest state to provide contrast from the close clutter found in the built-up scene areas. This serves their background purpose well and provides for a number of bridges and tunnels for the LLL miniature inhabitants to en-joy on their train ride. Sounds of bird songs randomly fill all the mountains automatically transferring the sounds among multiple speakers, camouflaged by trees, gives the audible appearance that the flocks of birds are indeed moving about. Occasionally, in the far distance, the sounds of steam trains climbing the steep mountain grades can be heard. Multiple speakers are used here too, as the sounds echo off the rough terrain.

A boy flying a tethered model airplane can be seen high up in a small field near the edge of a cliff. This vignette springs alive with the model airplane flying about at ever changing angles, altitude, and speed accompanied by the synchronized sound of it's tiny engine as it accelerates and glides.

Mole Hill Mine Company is the larger of the two major industries nestled in the mountain region. The rocks and soil here are most colorful. Red, orange, and yellow hues abound indicating the area the abundant of minerals in this region. The mine bores straight into a rich vein of iron ore in the side of Mole Hill Mountain. Two sidings from the LLL's Mountain Division branch line lead directly into the mine building to ease the task of retrieving the ore. The drilling, loading, clank, and clatter of the mining operation can be heard as the waiting shorty hoppers are filled to capacity. A snowplow constantly stands at the ready to combat sudden snowfalls, which are not uncommon at this elevation.

The coke ovens of the Mole Hill Coke Company may be seen across the tracks. These are of the old beehive design. Both the iron ore and the coke are shipped by rail to fuel steel company furnaces on the far side of the mountain. One can normally see a dim red glow inside the multiple coke oven openings. Guests may operate a panel switch to start a coke oven-charging scene. Activity abounds as the fires, now with bright yellow flames, flare higher and higher. The sizzling sound of the burning material is heard and enormous clouds of smoke stream from each opening! Gradually, the flames subside to the

A family hiking on Mole Hill Mountain discovers a breathtaking view of the Rocky River. The rocks below are from the real Swift River by the Kancamangus Highway in New Hampshire's White Mountains. A lightship (left center) warns watercraft entering the narrows via winking beacons along with bell and foghorn sound effects.

faint red glow, the smoke clears, and the mountains are again quiet. Only the sounds of the nearby mine work, bird songs, and low rumbling of distant trains are heard.

Near the base of the mountains, the Poppa Cow Dairy runs its operation. It has a loading platform to accept standard operating milk car deliveries. It features a continuously moving rotary milk can conveyor and a man who infrequently appears carrying a milk can to the waiting trucks.

Mainline trains stop at tiny town of Mousebelly nestled in the foothills of Bumpy Top Mountain. Here, I have located Mousebelly Station with its cheerful flickering fireplace. Toonerville Traction Company interurban trolleys stop at Mousebelly Station on a regular schedule to take travelers to and from the ever-popular Buena Vista Amusement Park.

Like the Podunk Traction Company city trolleys, I also consider the Toonerville interurban line to be an animation. It is a totally automatic system consisting of two track loops. A single work-truck trolley runs in a clockwise direction on the inner loop. It disappears into a distant tunnel behind the cliff, later to emerge and periodically stop by a rock slide area. A local work crew loads the truck with boulders that have fallen in close proximity to the tracks. Three passenger trolley cars operate on the outer loop in a counter-clockwise direction. These travel out of sight through a deep cut to the Buena Vista Amusement Park incline entrance on the opposite side of Bumpy Top Mountain. Combinations of one or two trolleys may be seen at Mousebelly Station at a given time. An automatic stop signal system controls the trolley's operation at Mousebelly. An overhead catenary system supplies power to the trolley car lights. This

feature allows them to remain illuminated when the cars are at rest.

All kids are naturally attracted to the Rocky River area. Babbling sounds are heard as the water tumbles about the many rocks on its way to the sea. Children can be heard yelling to each other as they swim, dive, and play with their inner tubes. Another child is busy flying his kite, which blows about as it catches the breeze. Fishermen try their luck beneath the railroad bridge. Lightning bugs blink and scurry about the bushes where the sounds of crickets, whippoorwills, and frogs can be heard in the evening. The row and sailboats in the harbor gently rock with the motion of the water as a fishing trawler attempts to tie up at the dock. A lightship can be seen and heard in the distance. Its flashing lights and boisterous foghorn warn approaching boats of the narrow channel entrance via the railroad bascule bridge to the docking areas.

The pleasant strains of happy acoustic music can be heard emanating from Albert Music Hall down the country road. An engaging mix of live country, bluegrass, and folk tunes is played during the show performances. Periodic intermissions occur where the din of the crowd may be heard over the softer recorded background music. This light and acoustically animated model reflects the ambiance of the real Albert Music Hall, located in Waretown, NJ. Actual recordings from the real Music Hall are played in the model!

Quick Bat Cavern is located directly across from Albert Music Hall. This cave is loosely modeled after the caverns of Luray, VA. There is a ticket house complete with restrooms and food services. A lighted path leads visitors to the cave entrance where they join a guide for their tour. Hundreds of stalagmites and stalactites illuminated with multicolored lights can be seen through the cave's opening. Animated bats, high near the ceiling of the cave, whirl to and fro in frightening eccentric patterns at varying speeds. Naturally, the caverns derive their name from the rapid motion of these resident critters.

High Bridge Station quietly resides in the furthest reaches of the LLL's country branch line. This station, using a basic Lionel Rico Station shell, contains multiple animations. The ticket man paces his office floor while the shadows of workers can be seen on the rear office's frosted door window. Meanwhile a continuing parade of ladies may be seen entering the station's ladies room. The freight house area is a beehive of activity too. There are men moving about carrying boxes, moving hand trucks and operating the rear storeroom door.

Scenic Theme Area #4: Amusement Park (Buena Vista Amusement Park)

Buena Vista Amusement Park is a very obvious and definitive scenic theme area. It incorporates some of the most sophisticated sight and sound animations on the entire LLL layout. The design goal for this area was to emulate older-style amusement parks where the rides are custom fitted to the natural hilly, rocky, and wooded terrain. Here, the rides operate on characteristic schedules. Bright lights, lively sounds and the feeling of fun and action is everywhere. Rides range from nerve wrenching to tranquil as these parks were made for kids of all ages. All powered rides are sequenced off and on to allow patrons time to enter and exit.

Upon arrival at the Buena Vista Station on the Toonerville Traction Company line, visitors disembark and hasten to the entrance of the Buena Vista Incline. Here, an operating two-car incline brings visitors to the cheerful walking light sign that adorns the park's main entrance high on the top of Bumpy Top Mountain.

Here, in the highest section of the park, the steam-powered carousel is one of the most popular rides. Painted horses move up and down as hundreds of miniature lights walk around the center panels while the ride rotates. Smoke belches from the stack of the adjacent steam powerhouse as the boiler fire must be stoked up to power the carousel. Music recorded from a real steam powered carousel is simultaneously heard. Across the path, a towering Ferris wheel briefly stops and starts numerous times to allow riders to fill each car, then runs for an extended period of time to give everyone their moneys worth. The adjacent pony ride features a top canopy, which quickly revolves in a direction opposite that of the slower moving ponies below. This, as com-

Buena Vista Amusement Park is located on both a high and lower plateau section of the Bumpy Top Mountains. A colorful, open-sided cable car connects both sections by shuttling visitors across a spindly wood trestle that spans the Toonerville Traction Company tracks far below.

monly done in real parks, gives small children the feeling that they are riding much faster than they really are.

An operating model of a San Francisco cable car connects the Bumpy Top Mountain area with a lower plateau area of rides where an operating wheel-of-fortune, haunted lighthouse, children's swing and moving balloon man are seen. A short walk leads all to the thrilling rocket ship ride and the pleasant Small World boat ride. The Small World has free-floating moving boats while its well-known theme music can be heard playing inside the structure. Animated figures gleefully move about the building's roof to entice people to try the ride.

Conclusion

Obviously, animations form a significant part of the Little Lakes Lines. I find them fun to conceive, build, operate and show to others. Most are far simpler to construct than one may think at first glance. Collectively, I believe that they add immense interest to the train layout. Many LLL animations from the Amusement Park, City, Country (a combination of the Mole Hill Mountains and Rocky River theme areas) and Railroad Yard are described in detail in the following chapters.

Chapter Two

Animation Electronic Control: Definitions & Construction

The basic single-loop electrical circuit concept is used repeatedly in accomplishing the projects presented in this book. It is the same concept used, perhaps unknowingly, by anyone who hooks up even the smallest of model railroad sets. You do not need an in-depth knowledge about the details of electricity to use it in these applications. Every circuit may be drawn as a single wire loop, that invariably connects three distinct categories of items. The "Item Categories" include (1) Power Source; (2) "OFF/ON" Controller; and (3) the Controlled Device as depicted in Figure 1. Nothing more. The most complex looking diagram merely consists of multiple versions of this same basic circuit.

Six "building block" electronic circuits are described in the following chapter. They are used either singly or in combination, as required, for animated scene control. Tables 1 and 2 define the fundamental electrical terms and symbols utilized in these diagrams and throughout this book. Definitions are purposely limited and tailored to provide you with the essential information for construction of your model railroad animation projects.

Electronic control circuit construction is not difficult if done in an orderly manner. General-purpose printed circuit boards of various sizes are available from most any electronic supplier (e.g. Radio Shack). They have pre-drilled holes with a multitude of ready-made printed wire patterns and are configured to accept standard integrated circuits (ICs). These boards provide a convenient platform for mounting ICs and individual components for the circuits described in this book. Time can often be saved by first making a rough sketch of your intended parts layout before actually fastening any of the components to the board.

Obviously some soldering will be necessary. Soldering is best done with a low wattage (35 watt) pencil-type iron using small diameter rosin-core solder. All connections should be clean and mechanically tight prior to soldering. Although the electronic parts used on these projects are not particularly delicate, reasonable care should be taken to not cook the components too much! If some solder should flow where it is not wanted, desoldering braid (also available from electronic supply stores) provides an easy way to remove it.

It is strongly recommended that dual-inline-package (DIP) sockets be used for both the #555 timer integrated circuits and the 12 VDC relays. These components are identified in Chapters 3 and 8. Socket utilization removes any possibility of damage to these components from soldering. DIP sockets retain the same pin configuration and polarity notch marking as the item that is plugged into them.

Finally, as with all things electrical, safety and caution should always be practiced. This is particularly true whenever you become involved with electrical potentials in excess of 25 volts. For example, you may wish to control a 120 volt synchronous motor through relay circuitry for one of the animations. You should take steps to assure that there are no exposed relay contacts or wiring in your finished project. Any such wiring should be enclosed in a plastic project box and appropriately labeled. Likewise, all wires running to the animation motor in the display should be properly protected.

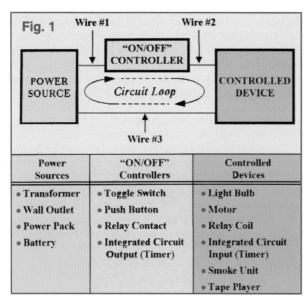

Power Sources	"ON/OFF" Controllers	Controlled Devices
• Transformer	• Toggle Switch	• Light Bulb
• Wall Outlet	• Push Button	• Motor
• Power Pack	• Relay Contact	• Relay Coil
• Battery	• Integrated Circuit Output (Timer)	• Integrated Circuit Input (Timer)
		• Smoke Unit
		• Tape Player

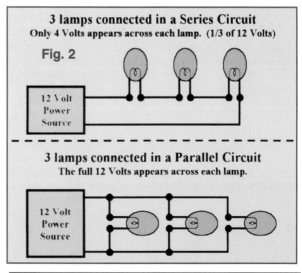

Left: Fig. 1: Basic Electrical Circuit "Item Categories"
Above: Fig. 2: Series & Parallel Lamp Circuits

Table 1
Electrical Term Definitions

Alternating Current (AC) - An electric current that reverses direction in a circuit at regular intervals. AC sources include your typical 120 volt house current in the U.S., which reverses direction at 60 Hz (60 times per second). It allows use of transformers to reduce house voltage to suitable levels for model train operation.

Ampere - An unit of measure of electrical current flow.

Capacitor - An electric circuit element used to store charge temporarily. (Uses include setting the time duration of electronic timer circuits.)

Diode - An electronic device that restricts current flow chiefly to one direction.

Diode Bridge - An electronic device for converting AC current to DC current.

Direct Current (DC) - An electric current flowing in one direction only.

Integrated Circuit (IC) - An electronic device containing many internal electrical elements to collectively perform a particular function. (e.g. electronic timer)

Parallel Circuit - An electrical circuit configuration where controlled devices (e.g. lamps) are connected directly across the voltage source (see Figure 2). Each device in the parallel circuit receives the full source voltage.

Permanent Magnet Motor - An electric motor consisting of a permanent magnet field and a wire wound armature. Permanent magnet motors operate on DC current only and are reversible. Motor speed increases as applied voltage increases. "Can" motors found in model trains are normally of this type.

Polarity - Related to various electrical device characteristics. Addressed herein as a "+" for a higher potential DC Voltage source with current flowing towards "-" or "ground". The "+" and "-" symbols also appear as important orientation markings on diodes, bridge rectifiers and polarized capacitors."

Relay - A device that responds to a small current or voltage change by activating switches or other devices in an electric circuit.

Resistor - A device used to control current in an electric circuit by providing resistance. (Uses include setting the time duration of electronic timer circuits.)

Series Circuit - An electrical circuit configuration where controlled devices (e.g. lamps) are connected end to end in sequence (see Figure 2). Each device in the series circuit receives just a fraction of the source voltage.

Synchronous Motor - A motor, which moves in phase with the electrical current that, powers it. They include an integral gearbox to achieve a single preset non-varying speed of operation. Synchronous motors operate on AC current only and are not reversible. Motor-driven clocks use synchronous motors.

Transformer - A device to convert AC voltage and current.

Universal Motor - An electric motor consisting of a wire wound field and armature. Universal motors operate on either AC or DC current and are reversible. Motor speed increases as applied voltage increases. Typical Lionel train open frame motors are of this type.

Volt - An unit of measure of electric potential.

Table 2
Wiring Diagram Symbols

Symbol Description		Symbol Description	
Connecting Wires (Electrically connected.)		**Relay: SPDT** (Single Pole/Double Throw) Consists of an actuating coil that is mechanically linked to a set of electrical contacts. The far outer contact disconnects from, and the near outer contact connects to, the center contact when the relay coil is energized.	
Non-Connecting Wires (No electrical connection.)			
Resistor Polarity is not important.		**Relay: DPDT** (Double Pole/Double Throw) Same as the SPDT relay above, but the DPDT relay controls two set of contacts.	
Capacitor (Non-polarized) Polarity is not important.			
Capacitor (Polarized) Polarity is important. "+" is the flat side of the symbol.		**Regulator - Integrated Circuit** Top View is always shown. Provides a predetermined constant DC (Direct Current) voltage level output over a wide range of DC input voltages. Both the center pin and the mounting tab are internally connected as the DC ground.	
Diode Polarity is important. Arrow points to "-"			
Bridge Rectifier Polarity is important. "+" is the long lead. "-" is always opposite the "+". "~" are the AC connections.		**Timer - Integrated Circuit** Top View is always shown. 8 Pin DIP (Dual in-line Package) The notch shown at the top is used to locate the pin numbers. Use of an 8-pin socket is recommended. The socket has a corresponding notch.	
Toggle Switch When switched ON, the connection stays closed until purposely switched OFF.			
Pushbutton Switch (Normally open) Push button to switch ON. Release button to switch OFF.		**Incandescent Lamp** (Light Bulb) Lamp shown with bare wire leads. Other common designs include miniature screw and bayonet bases.	

Chapter Three

Animation Electronic Control: The 6 Basic Circuits

Electronic circuits are often used to breathe life into the animations on the Little Lakes Lines. All animation functions described in this book are controlled by use of two basic circuit types. These are voltage regulation circuits and timer circuits (five variations). Fortunately, the circuits are not complex. Each circuit consists of from just four to nine components. No sensitive or critical adjustments are required for any of the circuits. Further, no real knowledge of electronics is required to build them. Assembly is a matter of physically mounting and connecting the specified components on a perforated board. Electrical term definitions, wiring diagram symbol identification and some general circuit construction considerations are presented in Chapter 2.

Descriptions outlining the fundamental purpose and use of each Electronic Control Circuit from a model railroad animation point of view are presented on the following pages. All necessary components and wiring connections are identified in the accompanying circuit diagrams.

Part numbers are identified from two sources for each component, at time of printing. R.S. = Radio Shack and M.E. = Mouser Electronics. See the Material Sources chapter of this book for address information.

Circuit #1 - Voltage Regulator

Model Railroad Animation Purpose:

Voltage regulators are used to provide electricity to other "electrical devices" at either a constant voltage level or as a not-to-exceed voltage limit. For model railroad applications these "electrical devices" may be lamps, motors, electronic timer circuits, or any combination thereof.

Components for Circuit #1:

The voltage regulator is schematically shown in the Circuit #1 Diagram. It consists of just four components. This circuit is capable of supporting either 5 or 12 volts DC voltage regulation depending upon which integrated

circuit (IC) regulator is used. The other three components do not change in either case.

Circuit #2 - Lamp Timer Type A

Model Railroad Animation Purpose:

The purpose of this circuit is to electronically control the lengths of time that a lamp, or lamps, will be powered. The lamp under control of this circuit will cycle more OFF than ON and can closely approach the point where the OFF and ON duration is almost equal. The lamp may be rapidly switched OFF than ON to give a flickering effect for fire flames or very slowly switched (i.e. for minutes at a time for special applications). This same circuit does it all! The actual time duration is determined by the values of the two resistors and one capacitor.

Components for Circuit #2:

The Type A Lamp Timer is schematically shown in the Circuit #2 Diagram. It utilizes the commonly available #555 integrated circuit (IC). This particular IC requires a bare minimum of external components for its operation. It operates from 5 to 16 volts DC. Most all of the Little Lakes Lines control circuits are regulated, (See Circuit #1), to either 5 or 12 volts DC.

Circuit #3 - Lamp Timer Type B

Model Railroad Animation Purpose:

The purpose of this circuit, as is the case with Circuit #2, is to electronically control the lengths of time that a lamp, or lamps, will be powered. The lamp under control of this circuit will cycle more ON than OFF, the opposite of Circuit #2. Again, the cycle can closely approach the point where the ON and OFF duration is almost equal. The actual time duration is determined by the values of the two resistors and one capacitor.

Components for Circuit #3:

The Type B Lamp Timer is schematically shown in the Circuit #3 Diagram. It utilizes the #555 integrated circuit (IC). You may notice that this circuit differs from Circuit #2 only in the location of the lamp load connection. Circuit #3 is usually powered by either a regulated 5 or 12 volts DC source on the Little Lakes Lines.

Circuit #4 - Dual Lamp Timer

Model Railroad Animation Purpose:

The purpose of this circuit is to electronically control the length of time that a pair of lamps will be alternately powered. They will never both be lighted at the same time. However, they can be adjusted so that each is illuminated for an approximately equal time duration. One will consistently cycle more ON than OFF while the other will cycle more OFF than ON. Actual time intervals are determined by the values of the two resistors and one capacitor.

Components for Circuit #4:

The Dual Lamp Timer is schematically shown in the Circuit #4 Diagram. It utilizes the #555 integrated circuit (IC). You may notice that this circuit is basically a combination of Circuits #2 and #3 in the lamp connection area. It too, is usually powered by either a regulated 5 or 12 volts DC source on the Little Lakes Lines.

The purpose of this circuit is to electronically control the length of time that a relay will be powered. The relay's contacts may be used to control electrical loads that draw considerably more current than the timer integrated circuit could supply by itself. (e.g. banks of lights and/or motors.) Relays are also used to control items, that require a different voltage than that used by the timing circuit. The relay under control of this circuit will cycle more OFF than ON. The cycle can closely approach the point where the OFF and ON time intervals are almost equal. The actual time duration is determined by the values of the two resistors and one capacitor.

Components for Circuit #5:

The Relay Timer is schematically shown in the Circuit #5 Diagram. It utilizes the #555 timer integrated circuit (IC). It is usually powered by a regulated 12 volts DC source on the Little Lakes Lines.

Circuit #5 - Relay Timer

Model Railroad Animation Purpose:

The purpose of this circuit is to electronically control the length of time that a relay will be powered. The relay's contacts may be used to control electrical loads that draw considerably more current than the timer integrated circuit could supply by itself. (e.g. banks of lights and/or motors.) Relays are also used to control items, that require a different voltage than that used by the timing circuit. The relay under control of this circuit will cycle more OFF than ON. The cycle can closely approach the point where the OFF and ON time intervals are almost equal. The actual time duration is determined by the values of the two resistors and one capacitor.

Components for Circuit #5:

The Relay Timer is schematically shown in the Circuit #5 Diagram. It utilizes the #555 timer integrated circuit (IC). It is usually powered by a regulated 12 volts DC source on the Little Lakes Lines.

Circuit #6 - Pushbutton-Activated Relay Timer

Model Railroad Animation Purpose:

The purpose of this circuit is to allow a visitor to momentarily push a button to activate an animated scene for a pre-determined length of time. Pushing the button immediately powers the relay. Circuit #5 will hold the relay ON for a length of time that may range from seconds to many minutes. The relay's contacts may be used to control electrical loads that draw considerably more current than the timer integrated circuit could supply by itself. (e.g. banks of lights and/or motors.) The actual relay hold ON time duration is determined by the values of a single resistor and one capacitor.

Components for Circuit #6:

The Pushbutton-Activated Timer is schematically shown in the Circuit #6 Diagram. It also utilizes the #555 timer integrated circuit (IC) and is usually powered by a regulated 12 volts DC source on the Little Lakes Lines.

Detailed component and fabrication information along with associated wiring diagrams are provided for each circuit beginning on the next page.

Circuit No. 1 - Voltage Regulator

Important Things to Know:

(1) The regulator must always be mounted on a heat sink to avoid excessive heat buildup within the chip, that could cause it to fail. Heat sink grease should always be applied between the regulator and the heat sink to assure good thermal contact for effective transfer of heat.

(2) The total electrical load on one regulator must not exceed 1.0 Amp of current. The current loading for each animated scene using voltage regulators is discussed in their respective descriptions.

(3) This circuit supports either 5 VDC or 12 VDC voltage regulation depending upon which integrated circuit regulator chip is used. All other components remain as shown.

(4) Input voltage may vary between 0 and 25 VAC. However, the output voltage will correspondingly vary until the input AC voltage is at least somewhat greater than the regulator's output design DC voltage.

(5) The bridge rectifier is typically 1.4 Amp, 100 PIV (Peak Inverse Volts) and normally packaged in a round configuration as shown below. Only the "+" lead is normally so marked. It is also the longest of the four leads from the device. The " - " lead is physically located directly opposite the "+" lead.

(6) The electrolytic filter capacitor is typically 1,000 uf and rated for 35 VDC or higher.

(7) The spike suppressor capacitor is typically .01 uf and rated for 50 VDC or higher.

Circuit #1 Parts Identification & Sources

Item	Number	Source
Heat sink grease	276-1373	R.S.
	524-8109-S	M.E.
Heat Sink for TO-220 type integrated circuit	276-1363	R.S.
	532-507302B00	M.E.
Bridge Rectifier: 1.4 Amp, 100 PIV	276-1152	R.S.
	583-RB152	M.E.
*5 VDC Regulator: (#7805) [TO-220 type]	276-1770	R.S.
	511-L7805CP	M.E.
*12 VDC Regulator: (#7812) [TO-220 type]	276-1771	R.S.
	511-L7812CP	M.E.
Capacitor: 1,000 µf, 35 VDC	272-1032	R.S.
	539-SKR35V1000	M.E.
Capacitor: .01 µf, 50 VDC	272-1065	R.S.
	140-PF1H103K	M.E.

* Note: Regulator is application dependent.

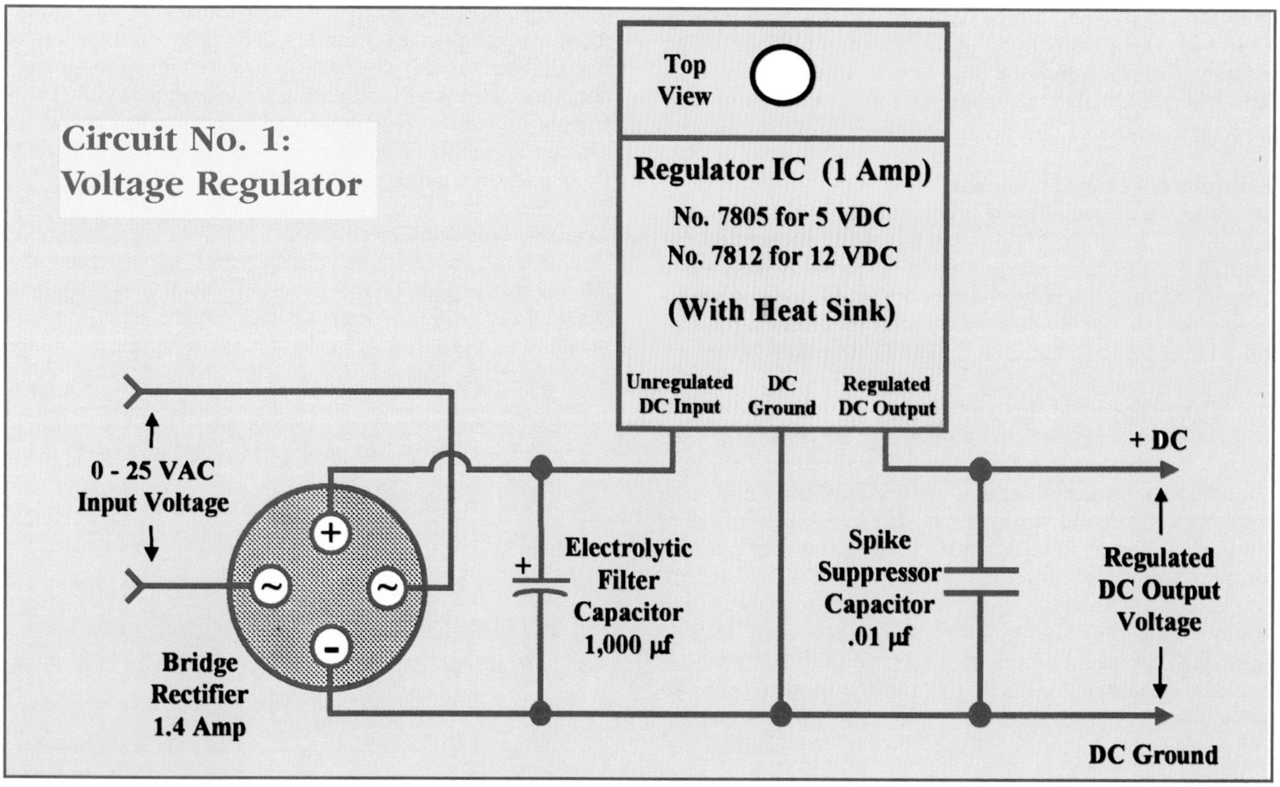

Circuit No. 1:
Voltage Regulator

Top View

Regulator IC (1 Amp)
No. 7805 for 5 VDC
No. 7812 for 12 VDC
(With Heat Sink)

Unregulated DC Input   DC Ground   Regulated DC Output

0 - 25 VAC Input Voltage

Bridge Rectifier 1.4 Amp

Electrolytic Filter Capacitor 1,000 µf

Spike Suppressor Capacitor .01 µf

+ DC

Regulated DC Output Voltage

DC Ground

Circuit No. 2: General Purpose Lamp Timer Type A

Important Things to Know:

(1) This circuit operates from 5 to 16 volts DC.

(2) The #555 integrated circuit (IC) timer can drive an electrical load of up to 0.2 Amps without requiring a heat sink. This is sufficient to control a number of light bulbs or most miniature relays without need of any additional external devices.

(3) CAUTION #1: Do *not use* the TLC555 CMOS timer in place of the standard 555 version. The CMOS timer does not have sufficient electrical load-driving capacity.

(4) CAUTION #2: It is advisable to mount the timer IC in a socket. The socket in turn should be mounted on a small project board for ease of wiring and assembly. (e.g. Radio Shack printed circuit board #276-150) Doing so will avoid the need to solder wires directly to the IC that could be potentially harmed by heat from the soldering process.

(5) Lamp OFF and ON duration is determined by the values of Capacitor C and Resistors R_A and R_B. The values of these components are identified with the animation descriptions where this circuit is used.

(6) The lamp will continuously cycle OFF and ON as long as voltage is applied to this circuit.

(7) The OFF time duration may be almost equal to or be longer than the ON time duration.

(8) All resistors are 1/4 watt or higher.

(9) Capacitor C is a tantalum type and rated at 16 VDC or higher.

(10) The .047 uf capacitor is a standard PC-mount type, rated 50 VDC or higher.

Circuit #2 Parts Identification & Sources

Item	Number	Source
Timer: #555 (Linear IC)	276-1723	R.S.
	511-NE555N	M.E.
IC Socket: Standard 8 pin	276-1995	R.S.
	575-199308	M.E.
Capacitor: .047 μf, 50 VDC	272-1068	R.S.
	140-PF1H473K	M.E.
Capacitor C: 16 VDC (Tantalum)	Application dependent. (See animation chapter.)	
Resistor R_A: ¼ watt	Application dependent. (See animation chapter.)	
Resistor R_B: ¼ watt	Application dependent. (See animation chapter.)	

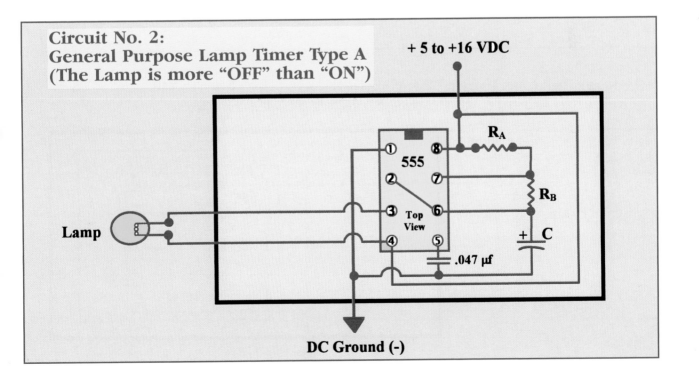

Circuit No. 2:
General Purpose Lamp Timer Type A
(The Lamp is more "OFF" than "ON")

+ 5 to +16 VDC

555 Top View R_A R_B + C .047 μf

Lamp

DC Ground (-)

Circuit No. 3: General Purpose Lamp Timer Type B

Important Things to Know:

(1) This circuit operates from 5 to 16 volts DC.

(2) The #555 integrated circuit (IC) Timer can drive an electrical load of up to 0.2 Amps without requiring a heat sink. This is sufficient to control a number of light bulbs or most miniature relays without need of any additional external devices.

(3) CAUTION #1: ***Do not use*** the TLC555 CMOS timer in place of the standard #555 version. The CMOS timer does not have sufficient electrical load-driving capacity.

(4) CAUTION #2: It is advisable to mount the timer IC in a socket. The socket in turn should be mounted on a small project board for ease of wiring and assembly. (e.g. Radio Shack printed circuit board #276-150) Doing so will avoid the need to solder wires directly to the IC that could be potentially harmed by heat from the soldering process.

(5) Lamp ON & OFF duration is determined by the values of Capacitor C and Resistors R_A and R_B. The values of these components are identified with the animation descriptions where this circuit is used.

(6) The lamp will continuously cycle ON and OFF as long as voltage is applied to this circuit.

(7) The ON time duration may be almost equal to or longer than the OFF time duration.

(8) All resistors are 1/4 watt or higher.

(9) Capacitor C is a tantalum type and rated at 16 VDC or higher.

(10) The .047 uf capacitor a standard PC-mount type, rated 50 VDC or higher.

Circuit #3 Parts Identification & Sources

Item	Number	Source
Timer: #555 (Linear IC)	276-1723	R.S.
	511-NE555N	M.E.
IC Socket: Standard 8 pin	276-1995	R.S.
	575-199308	M.E.
Capacitor: .047 μf, 50 VDC	272-1068	R.S.
	140-PF1H473K	M.E.
Capacitor C: 16 VDC (Tantalum)	Application dependent. (See animation chapter.)	
Resistor R_A: 1/4 watt	Application dependent. (See animation chapter.)	
Resistor R_B: 1/4 watt	Application dependent. (See animation chapter.)	

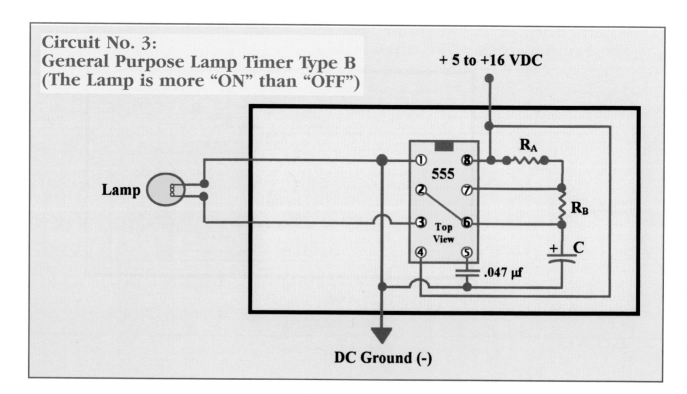

Circuit No. 3:
General Purpose Lamp Timer Type B
(The Lamp is more "ON" than "OFF")

+ 5 to +16 VDC

Lamp

555
Top View

R_A
R_B
+ C
.047 μf

DC Ground (-)

Circuit No. 4: General Purpose Dual Lamp Timer

Important Things to Know:

(1) This circuit operates from 5 to 16 volts DC.

(2) The #555 integrated circuit (IC) Timer can drive an electrical load of up to 0.2 Amps without requiring a heat sink. This is sufficient to control a number of light bulbs or most miniature relays without need of any additional external devices.

(3) CAUTION #1: *Do not use* the TLC555 CMOS timer in place of the standard #555 version. The CMOS timer does not have sufficient electrical load-driving capacity.

(4) CAUTION #2: It is advisable to mount the timer IC in a socket. The socket in turn should be mounted on a small project board for ease of wiring and assembly. (e.g. Radio Shack printed circuit board #276-150) Doing so will avoid the need to solder wires directly to the IC that could be potentially harmed by heat from the soldering process.

(5) The lamps will alternately light with Lamp #1 staying ON for a duration almost equal to or longer than Lamp #2. They will continuously cycle ON and OFF as long as voltage is applied to this circuit.

(6) Lamp ON & OFF duration is determined by the values of Capacitor C and Resistors R_A and R_B. The values of these components are identified with the animation descriptions where this circuit is used.

(7) All resistors are 1/4 watt or higher.

(8) Capacitor C is a tantalum type and rated at 16 VDC or higher.

(9) The .047 uf capacitor is a standard PC-mount type, rated 50 VDC or higher.

Circuit #4 Parts Identification & Sources

Item	Number	Source
Timer: #555 (Linear IC)	276-1723	R.S.
	511-NE555N	M.E.
IC Socket: Standard 8 pin	276-1995	R.S.
	575-199308	M.E.
Capacitor: .047 µf, 50 VDC	272-1068	R.S.
	140-PF1H473K	M.E.
Diode: 1N4001, 50 PIV (2 each)	276-1101	R.S.
	583-1N4001	M.E.
Capacitor C: 16 VDC (Tantalum)	Application dependent. (See animation chapter.)	
Resistor R_A: ¼ watt	Application dependent. (See animation chapter.)	
Resistor R_B: ¼ watt	Application dependent. (See animation chapter.)	

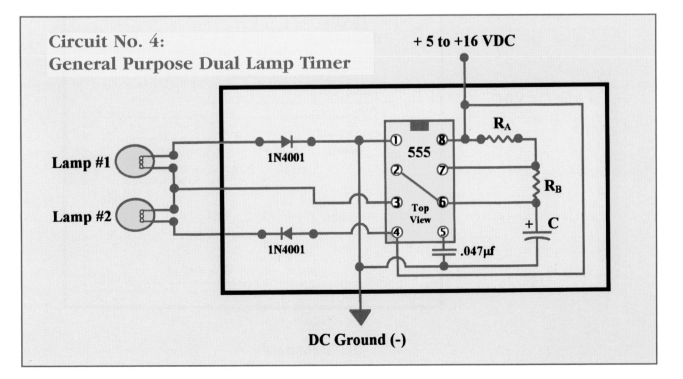

Circuit No. 4: General Purpose Dual Lamp Timer

Circuit No. 5: Relay Timer

Important Things to Know:

(1) This circuit operates from 5 or 12 volts DC.

(2) The #555 integrated circuit (IC) Timer can drive an electrical load of up to 0.2 Amps without requiring a heat sink. This is sufficient to control most miniature relays without need of any additional external devices.

(3) CAUTION #1: *Do not use* the TLC555 CMOS timer in place of the standard 555 version. The CMOS timer does not have sufficient load-driving capacity.

(4) CAUTION #2: It is advisable to mount the timer IC in a socket on a small project board for ease of wiring. (e.g. Radio Shack printed circuit board #276-150) Doing so will avoid the need to solder wires directly to the IC that could result in possible soldering heat damage.

(5) Relay OFF & ON duration is determined by the values of Capacitor C and Resistors R_A and R_B. The values of these components are identified with the animation descriptions where this circuit is used.

(6) The relay will continuously cycle OFF and ON as long as voltage is applied to this circuit.

(7) The OFF time duration may be almost equal to or be longer than the ON time duration.

(8) All resistors are 1/4 watt or higher.

(9) Capacitor C is a tantalum type and rated at 16 VDC or higher.

(10) The .047 uf capacitor is a standard PC-mount type, rated 50 VDC or higher.

(11) The 1N4001 diode protects the Timer IC from the back-voltage spike generated by the relay coil turn-off.

(12) Both the Timer and the DPDT Relay plug into DIP (Dual-Inline-Package) sockets.

Circuit #5 Parts Identification & Sources

Item	Number	Source
Timer: #555 (Linear IC)	276-1723	R.S.
	511-NE555N	M.E.
IC Socket for Timer: Standard 8 pin	276-1995	R.S.
	575-199308	M.E.
Diode: 1N4001, 50 PIV	276-1101	R.S.
	583-1N4001	M.E.
Capacitor: .047 µf, 50 VDC	272-1068	R.S.
	140-PF1H473K	M.E.
DPDT Relay, 12 VDC 280 ohm (or higher) coil	275-249	R.S.
	431-OVR-SH-212L	M.E.
IC Socket for Relay : Standard DIP, 16 pin	276-1998	R.S.
	575-199316	M.E.
Capacitor "C"	These components are application dependent. (See animation chapter.)	
Resistor "R_A"		
Resistor "R_B"		

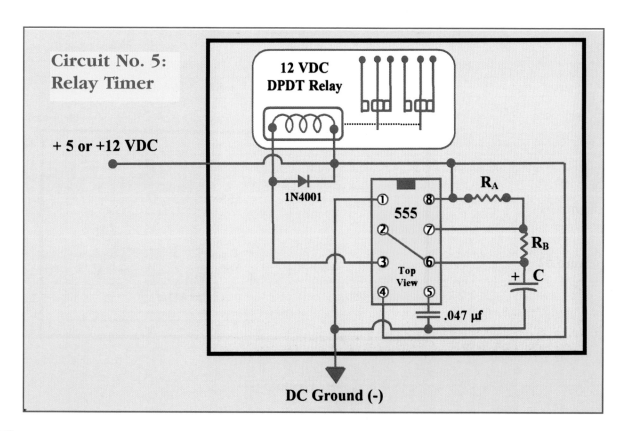

Circuit No. 5: Relay Timer

12 VDC DPDT Relay

+ 5 or +12 VDC

1N4001

555 Top View

R_A

R_B

+ C

.047 µf

DC Ground (-)

Important Things to Know:

(1) This circuit operates from 5 or 12 volts DC.

(2) The #555 integrated circuit (IC) Timer can drive an electrical load of up to 0.2 Amps without requiring a heat sink. This is sufficient to control most miniature relays without need of any additional external devices.

(3) CAUTION #1: *Do not use* the TLC555 CMOS timer in place of the standard 555 version. The CMOS timer does not have sufficient load-driving capacity.

(4) CAUTION #2: It is advisable to mount the timer IC in a socket on a small project board for ease of wiring. (e.g. Radio Shack printed circuit board #276-150) Doing so will avoid the need to solder wires directly to the IC that could result in possible soldering heat damage.

(5) Upon pressing the Start-Up Pushbutton, the relay will turn ON for a time duration determined by the values of Capacitor C and Resistor R. The values of these components are identified with the animation descriptions where this circuit is used.

(6) All resistors are 1/4 watt or higher.

(7) C is a tantalum capacitor, rated 16VDC or more.

(8) The .047 uf capacitors are a standard PC-mount type, rated 50 VDC or higher.

(9) The 1N4001 diode protects the Timer IC from the back-voltage spike generated by the relay coil turn-off.

Both the Timer and Relay plug into DIP sockets.

Circuit #6 Parts Identification & Sources

Item	Number	Source
Timer: #555 (Linear IC)	276-1723	R.S.
	511-NE555N	M.E.
IC Socket for Timer:	276-1995	R.S.
Standard DIP, 8 pin	575-199308	M.E.
Diode: 1N4001, 50 PIV	276-1101	R.S.
(2 each)	583-1N4001	M.E.
Capacitor: (2 each)	272-1068	R.S.
.047 µf, 50 VDC	140-PF1H473K	M.E.
DPDT Relay, 12 VDC	275-249	R.S.
280 ohm (or higher) coil	431-OVR-SH-212L	M.E.
IC Socket for Relay :	276-1998	R.S.
Standard DIP, 16 pin	575-199316	M.E.
Capacitor "C"	Application dependent.	
Resistor "R"	(See animation chapter.)	

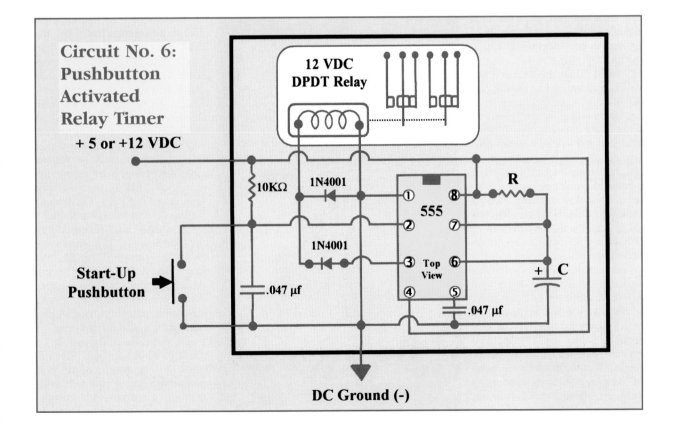

Chapter Four

Amusement Park Animations

The very mention of an amusement park brings the notion of a bright, lively, loud, and fun place to mind. Inclusion of such an area on your layout brings forth an almost endless array of animation opportunities! It also provides a convincing reason to operate your passenger trains. Each day hundreds of miniature people take the picturesque ride on the Little Lakes Lines passenger trains to the distant Mousebelly Station where they gleefully board the Toonerville Traction Company trolleys. A brief bouncy ride and they arrive at the Buena Vista Amusement Park incline entrance. They then embark on an all-day adventure at the park. A number of fascinating,

easy-to-model Buena Vista Amusement Park attractions are detailed in this chapter. There is the balloon man slowly moving about as his wares gently float above his head. Children are invariably attracted to the ghostly Haunted Lighthouse with its weirdly glowing gaslights and the playground swing. The Wheel-of-Fortune beckons adults to try again and again to win one of the stuffed duck prizes lined up on the shelf. Finally, for the thrill seekers, there is the stomach-wrenching Rocket Ride. Yes, construction of even the smallest amusement park on your layout can create considerable enjoyment for yourself and your full-sized visitors!

The Balloon Man

Everyone's face lights up when they see the balloon man coming their way. Balloon men were once a common sight at fairs, festivals, city parks and of course, as in the Little Lakes Lines case, the Amusement Park! A model railroad balloon man becomes even more interesting when you can see his fancy balloons gently wafting to and fro in the breeze! This is quite an easy animation to build. It can be created by a basic mechanical crank ar-rangement attached to a slow turning electric motor. An OFF-ON toggle switch is used to activate this animation.

Figure 1 shows the mechanical configuration of the motor, lever, and crank mechanism. This animation may be built directly on the layout table or as a separate assembly. As the motor turns, the crank follows for a while in one direction, slows to a stop, and then sweeps back in the opposite direction to the second stop position. The action then repeats. A low speed, about 1 revolution per minute (rpm) motor is good for this application. Balloon men were never known to be speedy!

The balloon man is a standard O gauge figure with a raised arm and standing on a base. The figure may be either plastic or metal. The balloons must be lightweight so that they can be affixed with a quick setting epoxy or cyanoacrylate bonding agent to the end of the 1/64" brass rod "strings" without causing them to bend. Small plastic balloons, or items resembling balloons, may be found as cake decorations in party supply stores as well as in a variety of general craft stores. The brass rod "strings" continue past the upraised hand and terminate in a drilled hole in the man's body close as possible to his other hand. They should then be bonded at both points of contact for stability. Now is the time to put any final painting touch-ups on the figure and the balloons.

A firm base should be prepared either on the layout or upon a separate assembly. The motor should be fastened in position and a crank rod bearing hole located as shown in Figure 1. Bend flat metal plate Erector #ME or equivalent, into the shape

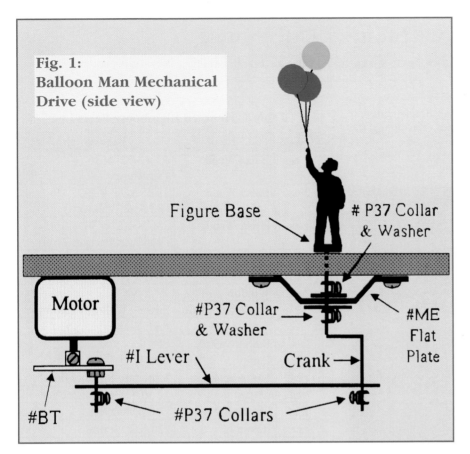

Fig. 1: Balloon Man Mechanical Drive (side view)

Figure Base

P37 Collar & Washer

Motor

#P37 Collar & Washer

#ME Flat Plate

#I Lever

Crank

#BT

#P37 Collars

long brass strip serves well as the lever. The length of the lever is not critical. Total movement of the man is determined by the distance of the drive pin from the center of the drive wheel and by the length of the horizontal portion of the crank in Figure 1. Installing #P37 or 5/32" O.D. collars on the drive pin and crank to secure the lever completes the project. A bottom view detail of the mechanical drive is illustrated in Figure 2.

Wire the unit to a power source and install a SPST power switch as shown in Figure 3. Place the unit on your layout, close the switch, and your balloon man is now ready to slowly turn to and fro as the wind catches his balloons!

shown and fasten it to the underside of the animation's base. This plate will support and retain the crank rod by the pincer action of the two #P37 collars and washers. The crank rod itself may be either an Erector crank #P24 cut to size, or formed from 1/8" brass rod. Insert the crank rod through the flat plate with the washers and collars positioned as shown in Figure 1. When properly aligned, the end of the crank should protrude about 1/8" above the ground level.

If practical, an interference size hole may be drilled into the base of the figure and the end of the crank inserted for additional mechanical strength. Quick-setting epoxy or super-glue is then used to fasten the figure to the crank rod. Everything must be temporarily held in place until the bond is secure. When set, the retaining collars should be adjusted so that the unit can move freely, yet not so free that it excessively wobbles during movement.

Assemble the Erector #BT drive wheel by mounting the 8-32 machine screw, lockwasher and nut. If the motor shaft's diameter should be too small, shims can be made by using brass tubing of the appropriate dimensions to obtain a reasonable fit. The #BT wheel attaches to the motor shaft with a setscrew. An Erector #I or a 5"

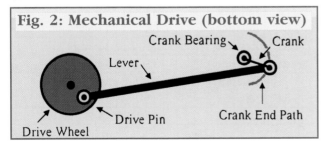

Fig. 2: Mechanical Drive (bottom view)

Crank Bearing   Crank

Lever

Drive Pin   Crank End Path

Drive Wheel

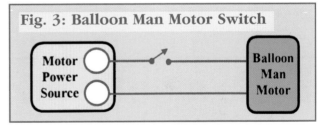

Fig. 3: Balloon Man Motor Switch

Motor Power Source

Balloon Man Motor

Table 1 Balloon Man Parts List

Quan.	Item	Description
1 ea.	Figure	Man with raised arm.
3 ea.	Balloons	Miniature plastic
12"	Brass Rod	1/64" Diameter ("String")
1 ea.	Motor	1 rpm with ≈1/8" dia. shaft
1 ea.	Drive Wheel	Erector # BT
1 ea.	Machine Screw	8-32 x 1" (Drive Pin)
1 ea.	Lockwasher	#8
1 ea.	Nut	#8
2 ea.	Washers	#8
1 ea.	5¼" strip	Erector # I (Lever) or 1/16" x 3/8" Brass
1 ea.	Flat Metal Plate	Erector # ME or equiv. (1/16" x 1" x 4")
1 ea.	Crank	Erector # P24 or 12" of 1/8" Dia. Brass Rod
4 ea.	Collars	Erector # P37 or 5/32" O.D. (1/8" I.D.)
1 ea.	Power Switch	SPST

The Haunted Lighthouse
(This Project uses Electric Circuit No. 1 and Three No. 2 Circuits)

Children approach the Haunted Lighthouse with fear and dread. Flickering gaslights guide visitors up the winding rocky path to the lighthouse building. A skeleton can be seen high in the tower when the beacon flashes on. A grizzled park attendant takes tickets to allow

entry to the haunted structure. Perhaps the scariest part of all is that there is no apparent exit! (It's hidden around the rocks in the back!) If you find your pike missing an amusement park, then consider installing a not-so-haunted lighthouse near a large lake or possibly an ocean at the edge of your layout. The lighthouse is most generic with the characteristic beacon tower and a small comfy side room for the light keeper.

Construction is simplified by the five-sided, as opposed to a round, tapered tower configuration. Basic structural dimensions are furnished in Figures 1 and 2. Major building components are identified in Table 1. Start by laying out and cutting the tapered side of the light tower out of 3/32" balsa. Then using this first side as a pattern, layout and cut the four remaining sides. It is most important that all five sides have the exact same dimensions. With the five sides in standing position on a

Table 1 Haunted Lighthouse Parts List

Quan.	Item	Description
1 ea.	Balsa Wood	3" x 3/32" x 36" (Structure)
2 ea.	Balsa Wood	1/16" x ¼" x 36" (Roof & Walkway)
1 ea.	Balsa Wood	1/8" x 1/8" x 36" (Walkway Posts & Trim)
1 sheet	Clear Plastic	Window & Beacon "Glass"
1 ea.	Door	¾" x 1 ¾"
2 ea.	Window	½" x 5/8"
12"	Miniature Chain	Silver (Walkway Railing)
-	Acrylic Paint	Red; White
1 ea.	Power Switch	SPST
1 ea.	Lamp	#1445, 18 Volts, .15 A
1 ea.	Lamp Socket	Miniature Bayonet Base
1 ea.	Circuit # 1	12 VDC Component Set
1ea.	Circuit # 2	Component Set
1 ea.	Resistor	220 KΩ, ¼ watt
1 ea.	Resistor	470 KΩ, ¼ watt
1 ea.	Capacitor	10 µf, 16 VDC (Tantalum)

Table 2 Gaslights Parts List (3 Lamps)

Quan.	Item	Description
3 ea.	Brass Tube	1/8" I.D., 2" long
3 ea.	Flat Washer	#4 Brass
12"	Tubing	3/64" Heat Shrink
12"	Tubing	1/8" Heat Shrink
-	Glass Paint	Transparent Amber
-	Acrylic Paint	Black
1 ea.	Power Switch	SPST
3 ea.	Lamps	#683, 5 Volts, 60 ma.
1 ea.	Circuit # 1	5 VDC Component Set
3 ea.	Circuit # 2	Component Set
3 ea.	Capacitor	2.2 µf, 16 VDC (Tantalum)
1 ea.	Resistor	5.6 KΩ, ¼ watt
1 ea.	Resistor	6.8 KΩ, ¼ watt
1 ea.	Resistor	10 KΩ, ¼ watt
1 ea.	Resistor	33 KΩ, ¼ watt
2 ea.	Resistor	47 KΩ, ¼ watt
1 ea.	Resistor	68 KΩ, ¼ watt
1 ea.	Resistor	100 KΩ, ¼ watt
3 ea.	Resistor	15Ω, ½ watt
3 ea.	Resistor	22Ω, ½ watt
3 ea.	Resistor	33Ω, ½ watt
12 ea.	Diode	#1N4001, 1 A., 50 PIV

Table 3 Circuit References & Electrical Values

Device	Reference	R_A	R_B	C
Beacon Timer	Circuit #2	220 KΩ (¼ watt)	470 KΩ (¼ watt)	10 µf (16 VDC)
Gaslights Timer #A	Circuit #2	5.6 KΩ (¼ watt)	33 KΩ (¼ watt)	2.2 µf (16 VDC)
Gaslights Timer #B	Circuit #2	6.8 KΩ (¼ watt)	47 KΩ (¼ watt)	2.2 µf (16 VDC)
Gaslights Timer #C	Circuit #2	47 KΩ (¼ watt)	100 KΩ (¼ watt)	2.2 µf (16 VDC)

Fig. 1: Top View (roof removed)

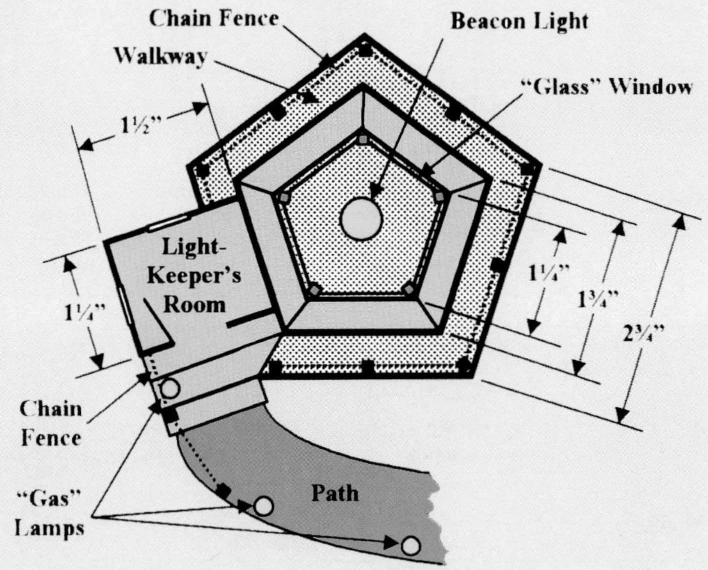
Chain Fence
Walkway
Beacon Light
"Glass" Window
1½"
Light-Keeper's Room
1¼"
1¼"
1¾"
2¾"
Chain Fence
"Gas" Lamps
Path

Fig. 2: Simplified front elevation view

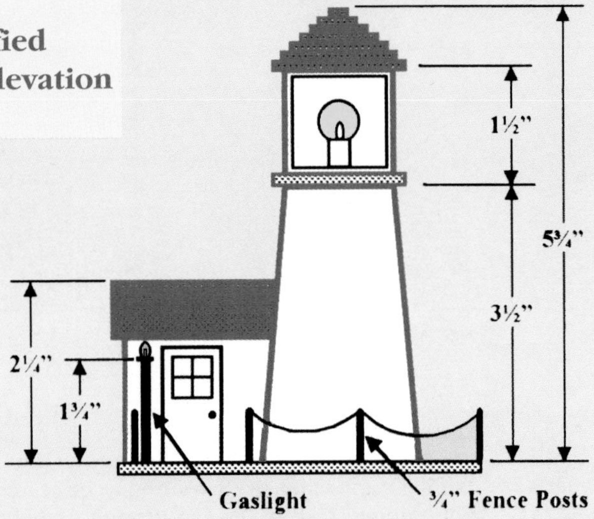
1½"
5¾"
3½"
2¼"
1¾"
Gaslight
¾" Fence Posts

flat surface, make any final adjustments and glue them together. The tower should be reinforced by gluing additional balsa strips inside. The little rectangular light keeper's room is very straightforward. It should be assembled next and glued to one side of the tower. The walkway may now be fabricated using the tower and room as its pattern. Measure and cut 1/4" wide balsa strips to form the promenade. Don't hesitate to paint the parts as you proceed. It is often advantageous to paint the balsa parts before actual assembly. Only easy touch-up will then be required when the assembly is completed.

A solid 3/32" balsa "floor" for the light in the tower should be shaped to overhang and generally match the angles formed by the tower's body. Mount a pre-wired, miniature bayonet base socket in the center for the light. Some reinforcing may be provided via use of balsa scraps. Frame the large beacon windows of 1/8" square balsa, mount as shown, and glue clear plastic in place. Insert the #1445 bulb in the socket. The beacon's roof is made of seven ever smaller five-sided layers of flat balsa. Assemble the roof as a unit. Fasten it to the large window framing with a couple of extremely tiny spots of glue. This way, the top may be non-destructively removed should the light ever need to be changed.

Figure 3 is the wiring diagram for the flashing beacon. Timer circuit component values are identified in Table 3. As the #1445 (18 volt) lamp will be operated on somewhat less than 12 volts from the flasher circuit, it is unlikely that it will ever require replacement. The brightness of the lamp is more than adequate for the beacon as it is directly viewed. However, if you really want to blind all the little people who live on your layout, a #53 (14 volt) miniature bayonet base lamp could be readily substituted.

A row of eerily winking gaslights along the path to the Haunted Lighthouse help contribute to the uneasiness of the miniature thrill seekers. It also adds an unexpected dimension of intrigue for visitors to your layout. Table 2 is a listing of the parts required for gaslight construction and control. The gaslights may be assembled as shown in Figure 4. Each bulb should be colored with amber glass paint to enhance the gas mantle glow effect.

Circuitry illustrated in Figure 5 presents a method to control three separate lamps so that they appear to flicker and glow in an irregular manner, somewhat independent of each other, to effectively imitate real gaslights. Their unsteady glow is purposely dim and wavering. Timer circuit values are delineated in Table 3. Each circuit provides voltage to the lamps at varying rates and intensities to achieve the effect. The diodes shown in Figure 5 are needed to keep the timer's voltage outputs independent of each other. Each lamp has a "by-pass" path consisting of a diode and a 33 ohm resis-

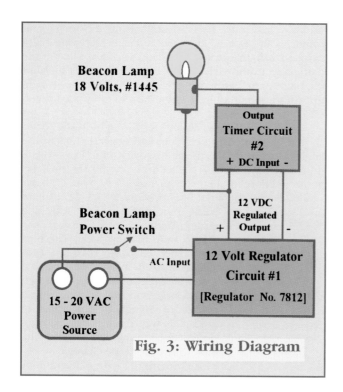

Beacon Lamp
18 Volts, #1445

Beacon Lamp Power Switch

15 - 20 VAC Power Source

AC Input

Output Timer Circuit #2
+ DC Input -

12 VDC Regulated Output

12 Volt Regulator Circuit #1
[Regulator No. 7812]

Fig. 3: Wiring Diagram

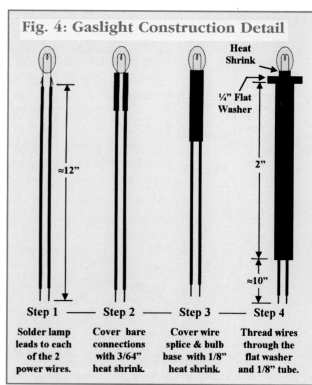

Fig. 4: Gaslight Construction Detail

Heat Shrink

¼" Flat Washer

≈12"

2"

≈10"

Step 1	Step 2	Step 3	Step 4
Solder lamp leads to each of the 2 power wires.	Cover bare connections with 3/64" heat shrink.	Cover wire splice & bulb base with 1/8" heat shrink.	Thread wires through the flat washer and 1/8" tube.

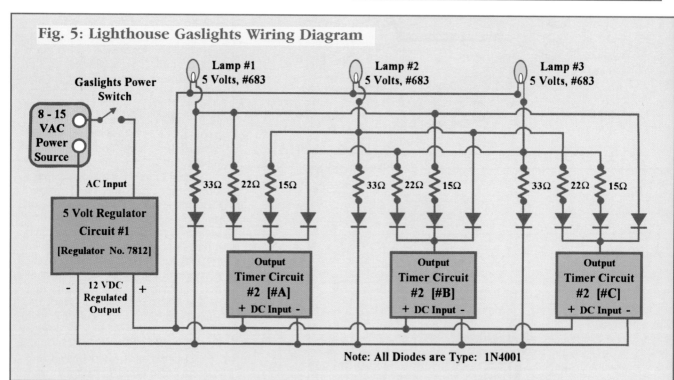

Fig. 5: Lighthouse Gaslights Wiring Diagram

Gaslights Power Switch

8 - 15 VAC Power Source

AC Input

5 Volt Regulator Circuit #1
[Regulator No. 7812]

- 12 VDC Regulated Output +

Lamp #1
5 Volts, #683

Lamp #2
5 Volts, #683

Lamp #3
5 Volts, #683

33Ω 22Ω 15Ω   33Ω 22Ω 15Ω   33Ω 22Ω 15Ω

Output Timer Circuit #2 [#A]
+ DC Input -

Output Timer Circuit #2 [#B]
+ DC Input -

Output Timer Circuit #2 [#C]
+ DC Input -

Note: All Diodes are Type: 1N4001

tor connected to ground. A minimum intensity lamp glow will be maintained at all times due to the presence of this path. The timers merely add the flicker effect. Alternatively, one or two timer circuits could be used in lieu of the three timers shown. However, noticeable deterioration of the independent flickering effects would be visible.

Finish the project by adding the posts and chain railing around the promenade. Scary skeletons, commonly found around Halloween in party and variety stores, may be added at various places to accentuate the spooky atmosphere. Add a generous-size gathering of families, apprehensively waiting to be scared out of their wits, queued up by the sputtering gaslights. Station a park attendant by the door to take tickets and meter the number of entering persons. Natural rocks may be arranged about the base of the lighthouse. An old rowboat perched on the rocks contributes to the nautical feel of the attraction and with its mysterious name "Devil" completes the horrific scene.

Family fun is the hallmark of the Buena Vista Amusement Park. There are all kinds of fancy rides for every age group. Many small children, however, head right for the swing set in a wooded corner of the park. There are few things as enjoyable as swooping through the warm summer air in the shadow of great shade trees. The children must take turns as there is but a single swing set available. (The Buena Vista's frugal management has intentionally limited the inclusion of charge-free rides.)

Swings make a very interesting animation. Their motion is quick-paced and obvious. A swing may be easily set up on your layout as very little space is required and it can be logically located in many different areas. Swings may be found in the backyard of homes and community parks as well as in large amusement parks like Buena Vista.

Table 1 lists the major components necessary to build a swing set. This animation requires about ten inches below the ground level for the mechanism. Some, very non-critical, soldering is required. With the singular exception of the wood seat, the swing is made entirely of brass.

Standard size brass rods are used to build the swing as shown in Figure 1. Two 1/16" diameter brass rods are bent to form the two side frames. Horizontal braces of 1/32" diameter brass rod are soldered in position on each side frame. A 1/8" diameter brass tube bushing is slid over the 3/32" diameter brass rod Cross-Support Bar. Each end of 3/32"Cross-Support Bar is soldered to the apex of each side frame, (See Figures 1 and 2). The brass tube should move freely about the Cross-Support Bar.

A 1/64" brass rod "Rope" is formed as depicted in Figure 3 with its two ends soldered to the Movable Brass Tube Bushing. Build and install the wood seat as shown. Next, make the Actuator Arm from a short piece of 1/64" diameter brass rod forming a small loop as may be seen in Figure 2. Allow about 1/4" of this arm to extend out and solder it onto the Movable Bushing. (Note: Alternatively, to ease soldering on the Movable Bushing, the loop can be made from an extension of the nearest "Rope" rod.)

Now drill a clearance hole for a 6-32 machine screw in an Erector #P7 Pulley or equivalent. This hole should be offset approximately 1/4" from the center of the pulley, (See Figure 1). A 1" 6-32 machine screw is then affixed to the pulley with a locknut and washer as shown. Place a #6 flat washer on next. Then slip a short piece of 5/32" I.D. Brass Tube onto the screw. This will serve as a smooth bearing surface for the 1" diameter Brass Drive Washer that is now put into place. Add a second #6 flat washer, locknut, and nut to secure the entire

Table 1 Playground Swing Parts List

Quan.	Item	Description
1 ea.	Base	Small piece of ½" Plywood
1 ea.	Figure	Seated Figure
1 ea.	Balsa Wood	5/8"x3/16"x3/32"(Swing Seat)
1 ea.	Brass Rod	1/16" Diameter, 12" long (Swing side frames)
1 ea.	Brass Rod	3/32" Diameter, 1¼" long (Swing top cross support bar)
1 ea.	Brass Rod	1/32" Diameter, 6" long (Horizontal side braces)
1 ea.	Brass Rod	1/64" Diameter, 6" long (Swing "Ropes")
1 ea.	Brass Rod	1/64" Diameter, 12" long (Actuator Wire & Arm)
1 ea.	Brass Tube	1/8" Diameter, 1" long (Moving top bushing)
1 ea.	Pulley	Erector #P7
1 ea.	Machine Screw	6-32, 1" long
2 ea.	Nut	6-32
2 ea.	Lockwasher	No. 6
2 ea.	Washer	No. 6
1	Brass Washer	≈1" dia. with ≈¼" hole (Drive Washer)
1	Brass Tube	5/32" I.D., ≈¼" long (Machine screw bushing.)
1 ea.	Motor	10 rpm with ≈1/8" dia. shaft
1 ea.	Power Switch	SPST
Misc.	Acrylic Paints	

assembly. At this point, the 1" diameter Brass Drive Washer should move freely on the Brass Tube Bushing.

Drill a small hole in the wood base for the Brass Actuator Rod to pass through. Position and mount both the swing and motor unit as illustrated in Figure 1. The motor should revolve at about 10 rpm to emulate a convincing swinging action. Figure 4 provides the wiring diagram of the motor circuit.

Form a zig-zag bend in one end of the 1/64" Brass Actuator Rod. Rotate the motor shaft to the uppermost position as shown in Figures 1 and 2. Feed the bent section of the Brass Actuator Rod through the Actuator Arm Loop. Align the swing in the left uppermost position. When the desired height of swing is achieved, solder the straight end of the Brass Actuator Rod to the uppermost surface of the Brass Drive Washer. Power the motor and see if the swing moves properly. A little fiddling with the orientation and length of the Actuator Arm may be required to get the exact amount of motion that you are seeking. No more than one or two drops of lightweight oil may then be applied to the top Movable Brass Tube Bushing and the Brass Drive Washer's bushing to assure smooth operation. The wide bearing surfaces of the brass bushings and minimal moving drive parts make this swing a very reliable animation.

The swing may be painted any color you may desire with regular acrylic paints. Caution should be used when painting to assure that paint does not cause mechanical binding by running under the top Moving Tube Bushing assembly. Painting the brass "Ropes" silver (chain) or a light tan (hemp) color will help make the swing set look more convincing. So place a young child figure on the seat. Have a few more standing by patiently waiting. Turn on the motor, and you can almost hear the screams of joy! This is one scene that even the most casual full size visitor to your layout will not miss!

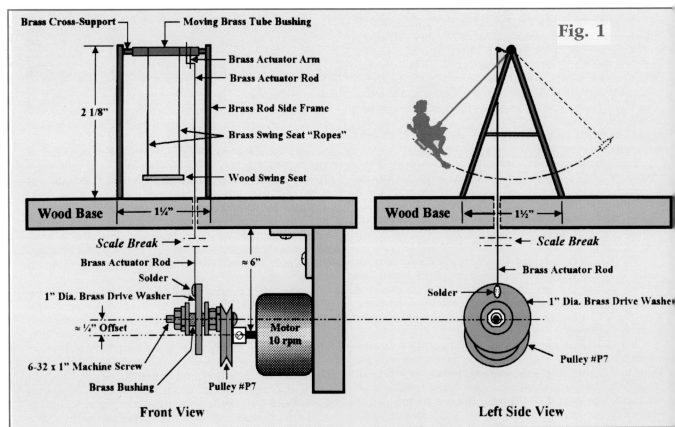

Front View **Left Side View**

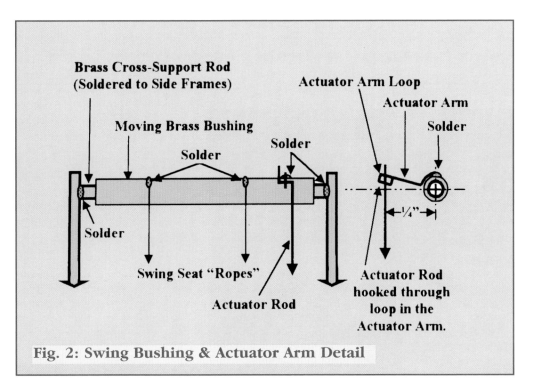

Brass Cross-Support Rod
(Soldered to Side Frames)

Actuator Arm Loop

Actuator Arm

Moving Brass Bushing

Solder

Solder

Solder

Solder

¼"

Swing Seat "Ropes"

Actuator Rod

Actuator Rod
hooked through
loop in the
Actuator Arm.

Fig. 2: Swing Bushing & Actuator Arm Detail

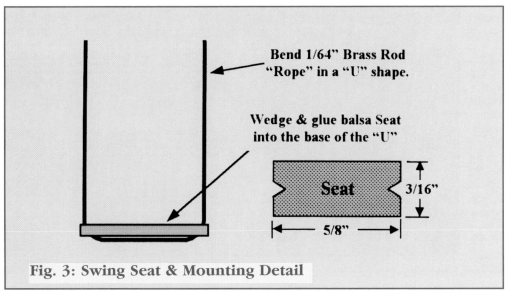

Bend 1/64" Brass Rod
"Rope" in a "U" shape.

Wedge & glue balsa Seat
into the base of the "U"

Seat

3/16"

5/8"

Fig. 3: Swing Seat & Mounting Detail

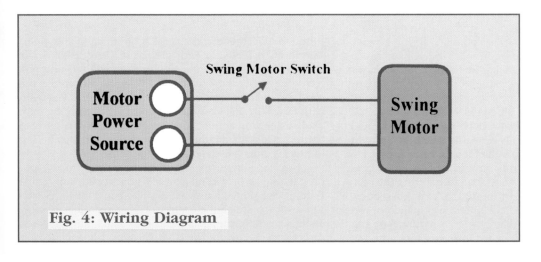

Swing Motor Switch

Motor
Power
Source

Swing
Motor

Fig. 4: Wiring Diagram

Rocketship Ride

(This Project uses Electrical Circuits No. 1 and No. 5)

The speeding Rocketships are at the absolute top of the Buena Vista Amusement Park's thrilling ride list. Their bright headlights and red taillights pierce the nighttime sky as they swiftly soar along to the stars. Locating the ride near the edge of a steep cliff helps emphasize the illusion that they really are taking off into space! The ride pauses occasionally to allow each miniature rider to enter and leave the sparkling rocket-propelled vehicles. When full, the ride rapidly accelerates as it proceeds to give each kid the thrill of a lifetime!

Major Rocketship Ride components are listed in Table 1. An overall view of the three rocketships used in this ride can be seen in the photograph. Each rocketship is made of balsa wood. They are about 4" long, 1" wide and 7/8" in height with exception of the tail fin which rises an additional 1/4". It is helpful to use some O gauge seated children figures as patterns to assure that your seating area dimensions are appropriate. The length of each support arm on the Buena Vista Park model is 2". Hub diameter is 1 1/4". These dimensions are not at all critical. Final sizing depends primarily upon the amount of real estate you have available for this attraction.

The head and taillights should be prepared and embedded into the balsa wood structure during the construction process. They are located as may be seen in Figures 1 and 2. Color the taillight with transparent red glass paint. Leave the headlight clear. Wires are then soldered directly to the #330 lamps in accordance with the wiring layout of Figure 2. Due to space limitations, it is best to use #24 solid bus wire (uninsulated) for this purpose. Be sure to dress the wires so that adjacent wires don't touch each other and cause a short circuit. Do all soldering *before* the lamps are placed in the balsa structure. (A soldering iron can quickly ignite balsa and glue!) Run the wire leads for each unit on the underside of the support arms towards the hub as shown. Each unit will have one ground "-" and one "+" wire. Complete the assembly which consists of the balsa wood rocketship with lamps in place and the support arms with the wire leads extending about 3" beyond their ends. This is also the most opportune time to paint the rocketships before the three units are joined together at the hub.

Figure 3 shows one approach to make a hub assembly capable of providing power to the rocketship lights. Erector Set pierced disk #BT provides a most convenient way to attach the entire rotating assembly of rocketships to the motor shaft. Support arms may be glued directly to the top of the disk. A round brass plate may

Table 1 Rocketship Ride Parts List

Quan.	Item	Description
1 ea.	Motor	Small, ≈ 30 rpm
6-12 ea.	Figures	O Gauge seated children
6 ea.	Lamp	#330, 14 Volt, 80 ma.
1 ea.	Glass paint	Transparent Red
2'	Insulated wire	Solid, #24 bus wire
1 ea.	Pierced Disk	Erector #BT
1 ea.	Brass Sheet	.015" x 4" x 10"
1 ea.	Spring Brass	≈ 3" long or relay spring contact to act as "wiper".
1 ea.	Power Switch	SPST
1 ea.	Circuit # 1	12 VDC Component Set
1 ea.	Circuit #5	Component Set
1 ea.	Resistor	470 KΩ, ¼ watt
1 ea.	Resistor	680 KΩ, ¼ watt
1 ea.	Capacitor	22 µf, 16 VDC (Tantalum)

Table 2 Circuit References & Electrical Values

Device	Reference	R_A	R_B	C
Relay Timer	Circuit #5	470 KΩ (¼ watt)	680 KΩ (¼ watt)	22 µf (16 VDC)

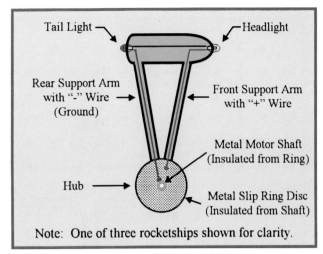

Figure 2   Rocketship Wiring Detail (Bottom View)

material sandwich may be held to the pierced disk via carefully insulated screws or even epoxied together. Non-metallic screws would also be a convenient means of fastening these parts together. Note: Erector Set insulated pierced disks were produced for this very purpose but are extremely difficult to find.

The arms from the three rocketships must next be epoxied in place on the pierced disk using care that the setscrew is not obstructed. (This setscrew in the pierced disk will eventually be used to secure the hub assembly to the motor shaft.) Ground wires from each rocketship should be connected together at the hub location and then soldered and/or clamped to the pierced disk. This forms the electrical ground path through the metal shaft to any metal area on the motor's case. Likewise, the three "+" wires from each rocketship should also be connected together. This bundle is then soldered to any available spot on the brass commutator disk. The "+" power path is then completed through the wiper, installed on a base plate for the motor unit, as shown in Figure 3. (The base plate may be either wood or metal. If metal, however, the wiper contact must be insulated from it via fiber or cardboard spacers and carefully located non-shorting attachment screws. The complete electrical path for the lamps is therefore maintained between the fixed base and the rotating hub bearing the rocketships. Install the base plate at an approximately 20° angle on your layout so that the rocketships can actually climb and descend.

Figure 4 outlines the wiring diagram for the control circuitry. Table 2 specifies the component values for the relay timing circuit. As shown, the ride is more OFF than ON. Loading/unloading the children is time consuming, whereas the ride is purpose-

be cut from sheet brass to form a slip ring commutator for the "+" voltage source. The brass will be configured as a round disk, slightly larger in diameter than the # BT pierced disk. This plate must be electrically isolated from the motor shaft ground via use of an insulating material. Electrical tape, balsa wood, or even cardboard would serve for this purpose. The brass and insulating

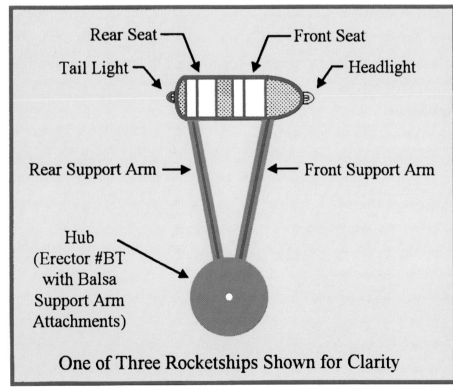

One of Three Rocketships Shown for Clarity

Figure 1   Rocketship Ride (Top View)

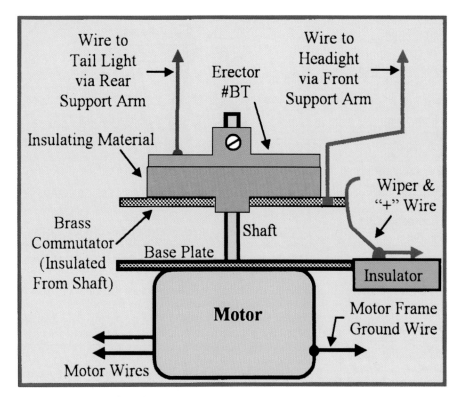

Figure 3   Rocketship Slip Ring Detail (Side View)

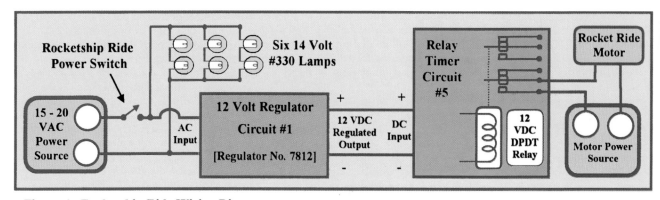

Figure 4   Rocketship Ride Wiring Diagram

ly kept short to prevent upsetting their tiny stomachs! The lights remain ON until the Rocketship Ride power switch is turned off.

Connect the motor and lighting wires from the motor and rocketship assembly module to the electronic control unit, install the power switch and your project is now ready for you to seat the 6 to 12 happy children into the rocketships. A flick of the switch and your tiny riders will be on their way to the great beyond.

Wheel Of Fortune
(This Project uses Electrical Circuits No. 1 and No. 5)

One of the big thrills of any amusement park is to try your luck at the games of chance. The Buena Vista Amusement Park on the Little Lakes Lines is no exception. For a mere 5¢ a try at the "Wheel of Fortune", visitors have the opportunity to win a beautiful stuffed duck! After they place their bet on a number, the wheel spins. If it should stop with the arrow pointing to their number, they have the choice of the stand! This animation is easy to build and can be a lot of fun to operate. Your full size visitors can place their bets too, because

Table 1 Wheel of Fortune Parts List

Quan.	Item	Description
1 ea.	Motor	Small, high speed
1 ea.	Pierced Disk	Erector #BT
1 ea.	Lamp	#330, 14 Volt, 80 ma.
1 ea.	Power Switch	SPST
1 ea.	Circuit #1	12 VDC Component Set
1 ea.	Circuit #5	Component Set
1 ea.	Resistor	330 KΩ, ¼ watt
1 ea.	Resistor	1.0 MΩ, ¼ watt
1 ea.	Capacitor	10 µf, 16 VDC (Tantalum)

Table 2 Circuit References & Electrical Values

Device	Reference	R_A	R_B	C
Relay Timer	Circuit #5	1.0 MΩ (¼ watt)	330 KΩ (¼ watt)	10 µf (16 VDC)

you never do know where the wheel will stop!

Tables 1 and 2 outline the major components for this project. Additional miscellaneous materials such as balsa wood, cardboard, glue and paint are needed to build the booth. It is a straightforward windowless, rectangular structure that has no critical dimensions. It is best to get your motor first and then build the booth around it. Most any small, high speed, low voltage, motor with an extended shaft end can be used. It can be AC or DC as it is controlled independently of the timing electronics via a relay contact closure, as may be seen in the Figure 4 wiring diagram. The motor may also use the same power source as the electronics if it runs satisfactorily on 15-20 volts AC. This is preferable as it eliminates the need for a second power source.

Once the motor is selected, it may be mounted in

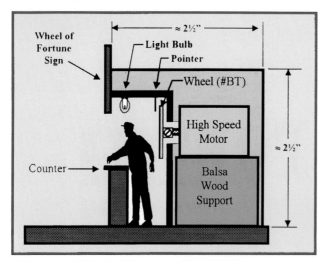

Figure 1 Wheel of Fortune (Side View)

Figure 2 Wheel of Fortune (Front View)

place on a base via gluing it to a balsa wood support to give it the proper height as shown in Figures 1 and 2. It should be centered about five scale feet from the floor. First construct the booth's wood back wall through which the motor shaft protrudes. A wheel may be made from white cardboard with a "pie-shaped" design drawn upon it, as detailed in Figure 3. The "pie" sections may be of different colors and/or contain numbers or words. It may then be glued to the face of an Erector pierced disk #BT as shown in Figure 1. This provides an easy

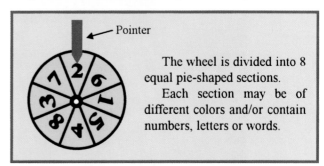

The wheel is divided into 8 equal pie-shaped sections.
Each section may be of different colors and/or contain numbers, letters or words.

Figure 3 Wheel & Pointer Detail (Front View)

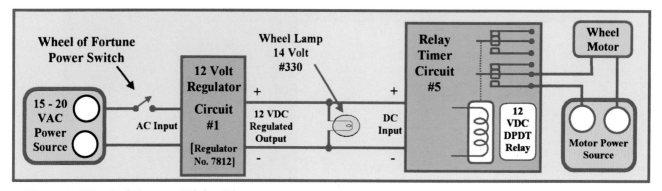

Figure 4 Wheel of Fortune Wiring Diagram

and positive means to fasten the wheel to the motor shaft. If a part, such as the pierced disk, is not available, you could alternatively punch an undersized hole in the center of the cardboard wheel and epoxy it to the motor shaft.

Now is a good time to finish the interior back wall before fabricating the rest of the booth. You may want to install shelves along this wall for the prizes. A pointer shaped from a balsa wood scrap should be positioned from high above in front of the wheel to serve as an indicator. It may either hang directly from the ceiling or be mounted on a wood spacer glued to the rear wall. Check to make sure that it does not interfere with the spinning wheel.

The entire booth structure may be made of a combination of balsa wood and cardboard. Complete the sides, roof and front counter of the booth. Install a #330 lamp overhead in front of the wheel to make sure that nobody misses the action at night.

Final detailing includes the placement of the prizes

on the rear wall shelves and an attendant to hand them out should someone win. The counter should have spaces marked on it to match each number on the wheel. Here the customers place their money in hopes of winning a prize duck! The all-important cash register should be conspicuously present on the counter. Attractive signs naming the booth, the cost to play, and the prizes to be won can be made with transfer lettering, decals, or could be computer generated. Naturally, there should be a large group of people crowding the booth to try to win!

Flip the power switch ON. After a pause for people to place their wagers, the great wheel of fortune will briefly spin. It then comes to a halt. The winner gets the prize, bets are enthusiastically placed again, and the wheel once more swiftly whirls into motion. This action sequence will automatically continue as long as power is applied or until they run out of prizes. Yes, you can almost hear the man behind the counter hollering: "Try your luck and win a duck!"

Chapter Five

The Animated City

Real cities are loud, bustling, lively places. Likewise, model cities should not just sit quietly in the background on your layout. They should and can project the feeling that some very interesting activities are going on. Trolley cars can rumble down the streets. A well-hidden speaker playing traffic sounds from an auto-reverse tape player is an easy way to set the general background mood. However, there are multitudes of foreground animation opportunities that can make a city scene absolutely outstanding!

A diverse collection of some most unusual and unique city-oriented animations are described in this chapter. These include a 20-piece band performing in a gazebo located in a central city park. All band players move about as the sprightly sounds of Sousa marches fill the air. A real smoke-puffing billboard mounted on a large downtown building is an indisputable attention-getter. There are moving dancing girls with boisterous music emanating from a local saloon. Ballerinas can be seen practicing through large windows in the local school of dance. Store windows pique the interest of the scale-sized city folk via moving window displays. Roy's Hobby Shop intrigues passerbys with an operating miniature train set. The train, complete with a brightly shining headlight and red end-of-train light, continuously travels in and out of scenic miniature mountains all within the hobby shop's front display window!

Continue on and see how you can create a city scene, that may develop into perhaps the most fascinating part of your layout!

Gazebo Band Concert

Band concerts are one of those pleasant indications that the summer season has arrived. The sounds of a stirring John Philip Sousa march may be heard filling the evening air in scenes that are repeated to this day in the "squares" of many towns and cities. Concerts are typically performed one evening a week. Usually the band is located on a raised platform. Audience seating, typically located on the lawn, often consists of portable chairs or blankets provided by the spectators. In our Podunk City gazebo scene, however, the organizers of this formal concert have thoughtfully provided the folding chairs.

Podunk City is fortunate to have this large gazebo, which can serve as a bandstand. The bandstand's basic configuration is shown in Figures 1, 2, and 3. Dimensions were chosen to provide space for a reasonable size, (20 piece), O gauge band and sufficient room to conceal a 4" loudspeaker in the roof structure. A 4" speaker is desired to support better reproduction of the band music. Locating the speaker in the roof of the structure, aimed downward to the band below, leaves no doubt to your layout visitors as to where the sound is coming from. The basic parts required to build the gazebo band concert scene are listed in Table 1.

Fabrication begins with the gazebo floor. This is made from a 1/4" thick aluminum plate cut into an octagon shape as shown in Figure 4.

Table 1 Gazebo Band Concert Parts List

Quan.	Item	Description
20 ea.	"O" Figures	Band conductor & musicians
1 ea.	Metal Plate	Aluminum or brass (6" square)
1 ea.	Wood base	1' x 2', ½" Plywood
1 ea.	Motor	10 rpm with ≈1/8" dia. shaft
1 ea.	Pierced Disk	Erector #BT
1 ea.	Glue	Balsa wood - normal drying.
2 ea.	Balsa Wood	¼" x 1/16" x 36" (Steps/trim)
2 ea.	Balsa Wood	1/8" x 1/16" x 36" (Lattice)
1 ea.	Balsa Wood	3/32" x 3" x 36" (Roof)
3 ea.	Brass Tube	1/8" O.D. x 12" (Posts)
1 ea.	Brass Strip	¼" x 1/16" x 12" (Arm)
5 ea.	Brass Rod	3/32" x 12" (Comb & cranks)
1 ea.	Balustrade	Turned, 6" (HO scale)
1 ea.	Speaker	4" Wide Range, 2 watts
24 ea.	Lamps	#330, 14 volts, 80 ma.
3 ea.	Power Switch	SPST
1 ea.	Cassette Tape Player	12 VDC with Auto-Reverse
Many	People	Seated & Standing
Many	Chairs	Folding
Misc.	Acrylic paint	White, Gold balustrade trim

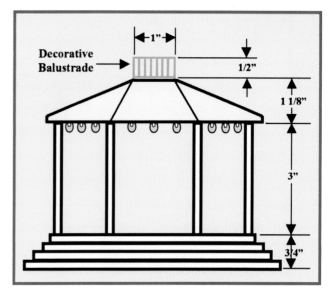

Figure 1   Bandstand Gazebo   (Front View)

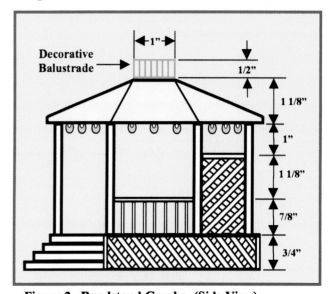

Figure 2   Bandstand Gazebo   (Side View)

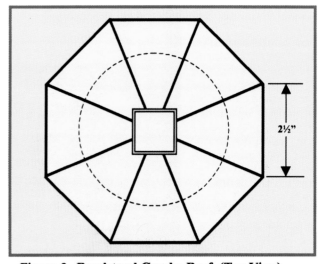

Figure 3   Bandstand Gazebo Roof (Top View)
Dotted lines show the 4" speaker position.

The floor must be substantial, as it has to accurately hold the moving mechanical cranks in alignment for each band member. Drill holes into the base to locate the position of each band member. As these holes, which will later serve as bearings for the crank rod assemblies, they should be drilled just a little larger than the diameter of the crank rods. Materials other than 1/4" thick aluminum, such as wood, can be used as an alternative. However, a good bearing surface, (e.g. brass tubing sleeves), must be provided for the crank rods.

A short brass rod is bent as illustrated in Figure 5 to form an individual crank unit. One is required for each band member. The dimensions of the bends are not critical. They may all be slightly different so that some band figures will display more or less movement than others. Each crank unit is positioned through a gazebo floor hole and held captive by soldering a metal washer, or piece of flat brass, to the protruding rod as shown in Figure 5. This washer will later be the base for attachment of the band member figure.

Next, make a 1/2" or heavier plywood base to support both the gazebo and the drive motor in accordance with Figure 6. A 10 rpm motor should be mounted in position as shown. A disk such as an Erector #BT or equivalent with an eccentric pin is attached to the motor shaft. The pin may be a short machine screw affixed to the disk with a lockwasher and nut. The disk and pin's purpose is to provide between 3/8" to 1/2" lateral movement of the travel arm for each complete motor rotation. Fabricate the travel arm of brass, shown in Figure 6, with a number of brass strip cross pieces soldered to form the double-sided "comb" array. Locate and install a couple of guide blocks on the wood base. Now is the time to test the movement of the travel arm assembly. Turn the motor ON.   The travel arm should slide smoothly back and forth as the disk and pin rotate.

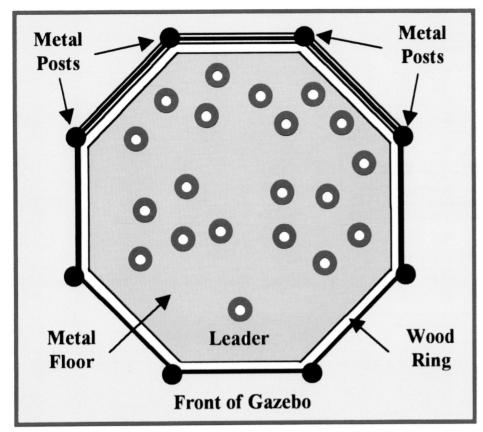

Figure 4   Band Position Floor Layout

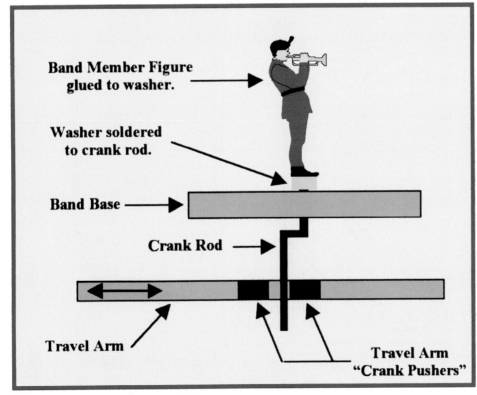

Figure 5   Band Member Mount & Crank Detail

Place a small pencil mark on the top of each gazebo floor crank assembly retaining washer. These marks will serve as an alignment indicator for system test prior to gluing the figures in place. See Figure 7.

Now position the gazebo floor assembly in place over the pre-tested travel arm "comb" as seen in Figure 6. Hold it temporarily in place with wood block spacers that do not interfere with the travel arm action. There is a bit of trial and error here as you mesh the hanging cranks with the comb's teeth. Some bending of the crank assemblies may be necessary to get everything working well together. Observe the movement of the pencil mark indicators. Each will move back and forth as the crank ends engage the moving comb teeth. Some will hesitate while others turn. All will swing through a greater or lesser degree of rotation. This is desirable, as each band member will move a little bit differently than the others in the group. It is important to make sure that the mechanism works smoothly now before proceeding.

When satisfied with the operation, permanently fasten the band base to the plywood base via wood blocks. This is a good time to paint the top of the band base while it is so assessable. Check operation again. Note the center point of the swing arc of each crank assembly using the pencil line marks as a guide. Mount the band member figures so that each faces towards the front of the gazebo when positioned at the center of their individual travel arc. They will not all face directly forward at the same time. Mount the conductor so that he faces the band at the center of his travel arc.

Now fabricate the gazebo

39

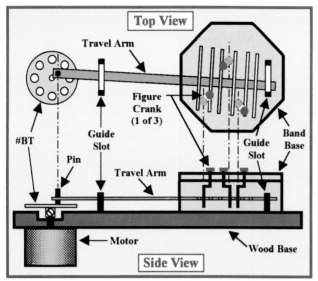

Figure 6   Bandstand Gazebo Drive Mechanism

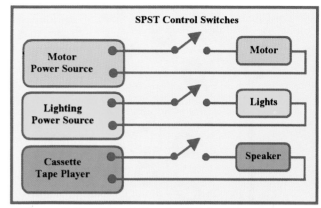

Figure 9   Bandstand Gazebo Wiring Diagram

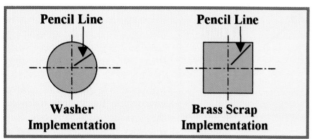

Figure 7   Alignment Indicator Marking (Top View)

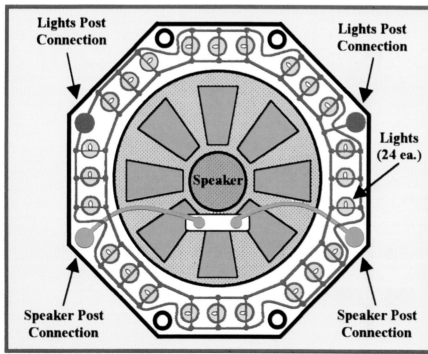

Figure 8   Gazebo Light & Speaker Wiring Diagram

around the completed mechanism. Start with the eight metal roof posts. Each may be attached by inserting it into a predrilled hole in the wood base. Be sure to keep them electrically insulated from the metal gazebo floor by use of balsa wood trim. Solder wires to one pair of posts to provide power to the lights located around the roof edge. The Podunk gazebo uses a total of twenty-four #330 lights. Three bulbs are located in each of the eight sides and wired as shown in Figure 8. The speaker is connected to a second pair of posts as shown.

Latticework consisting of thin, crisscrossed balsa strips with a top and bottom rail is placed between the main metal posts at the three rear sections. Sections adjacent to these each have a simple 3' high railing. The three front sections are open to the wide stairs. Additional lattice-work is located around the raised band base to conceal the mechanism. A statue in the park covers the motor crank assembly.

Figure 9 illustrates the wiring plan for the entire unit. Three separate switches are shown to accommodate the widely different power sources required for this animation. Alternatively, a 3 pole, single throw switch or relay could be used.

Insert a recording of your favorite band music in the tape player and then turn on the switches. Since more and more people gather as the band plays on, you should provide a wide range of spectators seated and standing on the lawn to complete the scene. An array of bicycles hastily parked along the side of the gazebo bespeaks the enthusiasm of their riders to see and hear the band. The conductor and each band musician independently moves about as their music fills the air. Sit a spell, lean back, watch, listen, and enjoy the show!

Smoking Billboard
(This Project uses Electrical Circuits No. 1 and No. 5)

What better way to promote your product than to display it on a huge billboard facing the town square park. Better yet, why not have your billboard be truly different from all the rest? Marketing people in Podunk City have taken a lesson from New York City's Times Square. There, years ago, a large billboard advertisement showed a man smoking a cigarette with real smoke puffing out. The sign even occasionally blew smoke rings! Due to changing times, this same billboard has been converted to advertising coffee with real steam coming out of the top of the cup. But as Podunk City is rather suspended in the 1950-60 era time frame, the local marketing men elected to go with a cigarette ad.

A model billboard that puffs smoke is not difficult to make and it sure will command the attention of your visitors. Table 1 identifies the main parts required to complete this project. The very first step is to find an advertisement to place on your billboard. Look through magazines to find a clear, full color picture of someone smoking a cigarette. It should fit within the typical billboard dimensions of 4 1/2" by 2 1/2". Once found, the picture should be cut out and fastened to a stiff cardboard backing using a thin layer of white glue. Next, glue the picture and cardboard assembly to a piece of 3/32" thick balsa wood for a firm backing as may be seen in Figure 1. (The Podunk City billboard is mounted directly on the face of a building making it easy to hide the mechanism.)

Drill a 1/8" diameter hole through the entire assembly in the appropriate spot from where the smoke should emerge. Insert a short piece of 1/8" brass tubing to assure that the hole remains clear. Bore

Table 1   Smoking Billboard Parts List

Quan.	Item	Description
1 ea.	Picture	≈2½"x 4½"
1 ea.	Cardstock	Smooth , heavy, ≈2½"x 4½"
1 ea.	Fan	4" Square, 120 VAC
1 ea.	Funnel	Large diameter to match fan.
1 ea.	Rubber Tubing	½" O. D., ≈1 foot length
1 ea.	Copper Pipe	½" I.D., ≈6"
1 ea.	Copper Pipe Tee	½" I.D.
1 ea.	Balsa Wood	≈1"x 2" x 3" Block
1 ea.	Balsa Wood	≈4"x 6"x 3/32"
1 ea.	Brass Tube	1/8"x 1" long
2 ea.	Brass Tube	3/32" O.D. x 3" long
1 ea.	Glass Jar	≈10 FL Oz. w/Screw Lid
1 ea.	Wire-wound Smoke Unit	Nichrome wire or heater resistor if space permits.
1 ea.	Kerosene Lamp Wick	Fiberglass ≈6" length by ½" wide.
2 ea.	Lamp	16 Volt Grain-of-Wheat
1 ea.	Project Box	All plastic, ≈ 7"x 4"x 2½"
1 ea.	Power Switch	SPST
1 ea.	Circuit # 1	12 VDC Component Set
1 ea.	Circuit # 5	Component Set
1 ea.	Resistor	820 KΩ, ¼ watt
1 ea.	Resistor	330 KΩ, ¼ watt
1 ea.	Capacitor	10 µf, 16 VDC (Tantalum)

Table 2   Circuit References & Electrical Values

Device	Reference	R_A	R_B	C
Fan Timer	Circuit #5	820 KΩ (¼ watt)	330 KΩ (¼ watt)	10 µf (16 VDC)

a 1/2" diameter hole through a 1" thick, 2" x 3" rough-cut balsa block. Insert a 1 1/2" section of 1/2" I.D. copper pipe in the opening, retain it with epoxy, and glue the assembly to the balsa backing of the billboard as illustrated in Figure 1. Be sure to center the 1/8" brass tube with respect to the 1/2" pipe as shown for optimum smoke transfer. This arrangement will permit for easy subsequent connection of the billboard with the smoke generator unit via use of 1/2" O.D. rubber tubing.

Next, drill two 3/32" diameter holes just above the billboard's frame for light support arms. Insert a 3/32" brass tube in each so that they extend beyond the front of the picture by approximately 1". Fasten and electrically connect a 16 volt grain-of-wheat lamp to each support by soldering one lead to the end of the brass rod. Solder a length of wire to the back end of the rod to allow for later connection to the power supply. Now, when all soldering is done on both ends of the rod as indicated in Figure 1, proceed to thread an insulated wire through the center of the rod. Solder this wire to the lamp's other lead. Make sure that the center wire remains insulated from the brass.

Figure 2 details the construction of the smoke generation system. A 4" square equipment fan is affixed so that its entire airflow will be directed through the small end of a funnel. The fan may be mounted to the funnel in a variety of ways depending upon their individual configurations. Screw clamps, epoxy, etc. may be used. It is important however, that the mating surfaces be sealed so that all of the air will blow through the funnel. The area where the funnel mates with the 1/2" copper tee should likewise be well sealed.

Smoke generator fabrication begins with making three holes in a jar's lid. A large center hole for the wick and two smaller holes for the wires. A 1 1/2" section of 1/2" copper pipe is soldered over the center hole of the lid. Be sure to clean the lid with emery paper so that it will hold the solder. At least a 125 watt soldering gun should be used for this operation. The smoke element heater may be a commercial heater resistor or custom made by wrapping a short length of nichrome wire around a fiberglass wick. The fiberglass wick is required in either case. The wick should be long enough to reach beyond the bottom of the jar. Note that filling the jar about 1/3 full of fluid, this tightly capped bottle system will provide smoking capability for many years without need of refill. Connect the 1/2" copper pipe into the bottom of the tee as shown in Figure 2. This joint may be sealed with electrical tape. Solder or tape another short

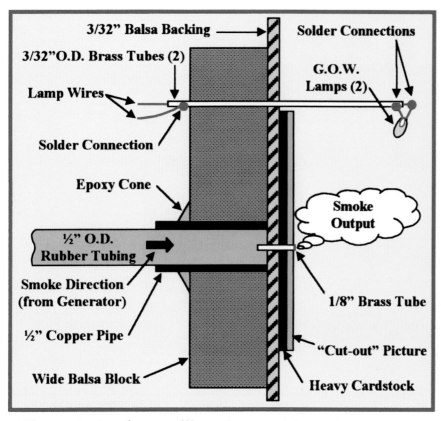

Figure 1   Smoking Billboard Assembly (Side View)

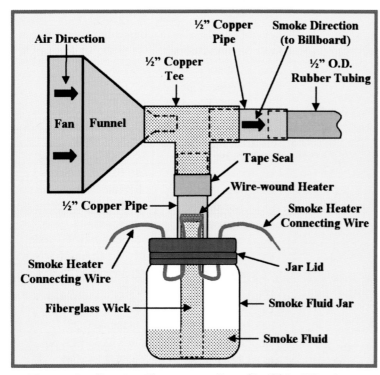

Figure 2   Smoke Generator Detail (Side View)

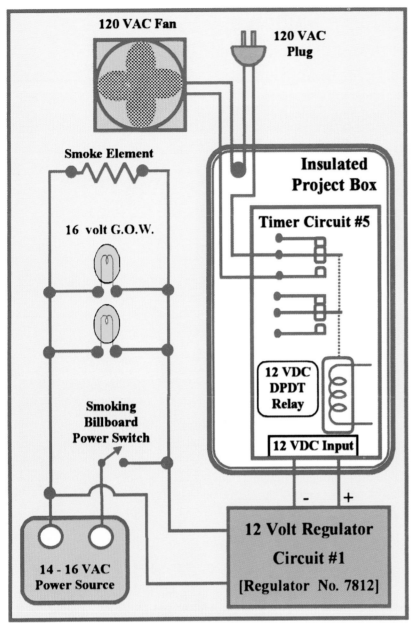

Figure 3 Smoking Billboard Wiring Diagram

Labels within the diagram:

120 VAC Fan

120 VAC Plug

Smoke Element

16 volt G.O.W.

Insulated Project Box

Timer Circuit #5

12 VDC DPDT Relay

12 VDC Input

Smoking Billboard Power Switch

14 - 16 VAC Power Source

12 Volt Regulator Circuit #1

[Regulator No. 7812]

- +

length of 1/2" I.D. copper pipe to the smoke output side of the tee.

Connect the generator assembly to the billboard unit with a length of 1/2" O.D. rubber hose. Hose length should not exceed 1' for best smoke-puffing results.

Figure 3 illustrates the wiring scheme. For safety, be sure to mount all 120 VAC fan connections in a clearly marked insulated box. (Lower capacity 12 VDC fans are also available and should work reasonably well if you wish to avoid the 120 VAC wiring.) Timer circuit #5 is used to pulse the fan on and off for the "puffing" action. In operation, the fan will most likely never come to a complete stop. It is desirable to keep a little positive air pressure in the system so that the smoke is always more than ready to spurt out when power is reapplied. If desired, you can vary the fan ON/OFF times, and thereby the smoking action, by changing the value of the resistors in the timing circuit. In general, larger resistance values will make both the ON and OFF times longer.

Test the unit on the bench to make sure that the smoke puffs are acceptable. If so, proceed to install it in your town. It is sure to get a lot of notice from your full size visitors as well as your O gauge town people.

When the building flats are removed, this is what can be found behind them (not an especially attractive sight, but then most behind-the-scenes vistas aren't). The black tube in the right foreground connects to the "cigarette" in the billboard. The jar holding the smoke heater element and smoke fluid is in the center and the fan is to the left.

Finn's Saloon

(This Project uses Electrical Circuit No. 5)

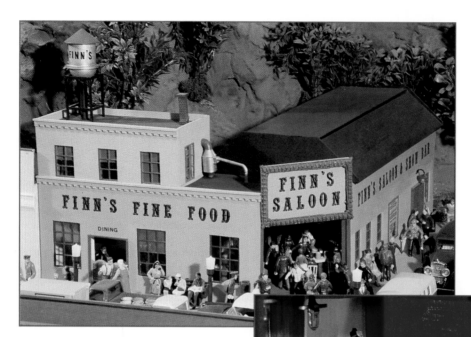

Every town has its rowdy side and Podunk City is no exception. Here, directly across from the Little Lakes Lines main passenger and freight terminals we have Finn's Saloon. It is complete with a mirrored bar, tables, and a lively music show. Miss Lanie is the featured vocalist who sashays about the small stage area belting out old time tunes with Miss Kitty singing harmony. Mickey who pounds out melodies on an old upright piano along with other energetic musicians accompanies them. The singers are dressed in flapper gowns while the musicians and bartenders are decked out in their spiffy red and white-stripped shirts. There are over 40 customers in Finn's singing and clapping along with the happy songs!

While Finn's Saloon is custom-tailored to a corner location in Podunk City, you can easily set up a similar establishment in any reasonably sized structure. Saloon-style ambiance is enhanced by the crowded interior, the mirrored bar, dim room lighting, and realistic stage lighting complete with footlights, blue background lighting, and a white spotlight on Miss Lanie. Table 1 identifies the major components of the saloon.

A sturdy building base is essential. Finn's Saloon floor plan is presented in Figure 1. Figure 2 illustrates a side view detail of the raised stage, animation drive and lighting. Locate the best placement for your stage. Be sure to arrange it so that visitors can easily peer into the saloon when it is installed on your layout. Stage position will inherently dictate the placement of the motor and dancer mechanism.

It is best to fabricate the dancer mechanism and have it operating smoothly prior to constructing the

building. An Erector #BT pierced disk may be attached to a motor shaft per Figure 3. A 1/16" thick, 1/4" wide brass strip makes a good travel arm. It may be readily bent to engage a pin (8-32 machine screw retained via a lockwasher and nut) from the pierced disk. A second brass strip should be bent as shown in Figure 2 to ride just above the top of the stage platform. This may be soldered in place on the main travel arm. Miss Lanie will later be affixed to this piece of metal. The main travel arm continues to slide too and fro beneath the platform as the motor turns. It should ride through a metal guide block as depicted in Figure 3. This block can be fabricated from a short brass strip bent into a "U" shape. The distance between the two "forks" of the "U" will greatly influence the degree of movement. Use trial and error in positioning the guide block with the motor running to get the proper amount of "dancing" motion that is appropriate for your stage area.

When the mechanism is functioning properly, the stage may be built. This is the time to install the "foot-

Table 1   Finn's Saloon Parts List

Quan.	Item	Description
1 ea.	Plywood Base	11½"x 15"x ½"
1 ea.	Balsa Wood	3/32"x3"x 36" (as required)
6 ea.	Windows	1" x 1 5/8"
1 ea.	Figure	Miss Lanie (Dancing)
1 ea.	Figure	Miss Kitty (Standing)
2 ea.	Figure	Standing musicians
1 ea.	Figure	Seated piano player
40 ea.	Figure	Saloon patrons
1 ea.	Piano	Balsa wood pieces
21 ea.	Chair	Piano player & saloon tables
5 ea.	Tables	Saloon tables
2 ea.	Pocket mirror	2" x 3"
1 ea.	Red Cloth	6" x 3" (Curtain)
1 ea.	Motor	10 rpm
1 ea.	Machine Screw	8-32, 1" (Pin)
1 ea.	Nut	8-32
1 ea.	Lockwasher	#8
1 ea.	Brass Strip	1/16"x ¼"x 12"
1 ea.	Erector	#BT, Pierced disk
1 ea.	Speaker	4" Wide range, 2 watts
1 ea.	Blue cellophane	5¾"x 3"
6 ea.	Flat Washers	#4 (House light shades)
14 ea.	Lamp	#683, 5 volt, 60 ma.
2 ea.	Lamp	#55, 7 volt, .41 A
2 ea.	Lamp	#44, 6.3 volt, .25 A
4 ea.	Lamp Socket	Miniature bayonet base
70 ea.	LEDs	≈.1" dia, red
1 ea.	Connector	6 pin polarized male
1 ea.	Connector	6 pin polarized female
1 ea.	Circuit #5	Component Set
1 ea.	Resistor	10Ω, 3 watts
2 ea.	Resistor	40Ω, 5 watts
1 ea.	Resistor	470 KΩ
1 ea.	Resistor	100 KΩ
1 ea.	Capacitor	2.2 µf (Tantalum)
3 ea.	Power Switch	SPST
1 ea.	Cassette Tape Player	12 VDC with auto-reverse

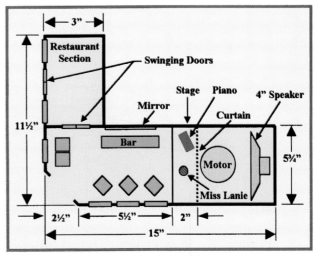

Figure 1   Finn's Saloon Floor Plan

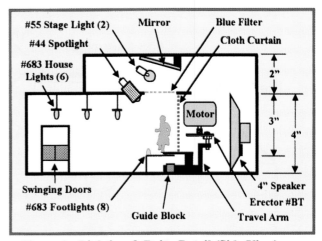

Figure 2   Lighting & Drive Detail (Side View)

Table 2   Circuit References & Electrical Values

Device	Reference	R_A	R_B	C
Sign Timer	Circuit #5	470 KΩ (¼ watt)	100 KΩ (¼ watt)	2.2 µf (16 VDC)

lights". Very reliable lamps are used here, as it is quite difficult to replace them when the building is built around them! These lights are subminiature 5 volt #683 lamps wired in series pairs. Therefore each pair of lamps electrically acts as a single 10 volt lamp. These series pairs are then wired in parallel as seen in Figure 5. This is purposely done so when the lamps are operated from a 6 volt source, they will glow with low brightness, run cool and will last a lifetime or two! The wire leads should be routed along a wall to the rear past the motor. Install the 4" speaker at this time. An exit for wiring may be made now either through the floor or later through an unseen exterior wall.

Build the walls of the building next using 3/32" sheet balsa. Paint or wallpaper the room. Yes, wallpaper with diminutive prints, as used in dollhouses, is an interesting alternative to painting. Remember that your full-sized visitors will closely inspect this room! Now is the time to assemble an old upright piano out of balsa wood. Attach Miss Lanie to the moving arm. Place Miss Kitty and the musicians in their appropriate positions on the stage (See Figure 4). Hang a red curtain backdrop toward the rear of the stage. The curtain will also allow the sound from the speaker to project forward. Tables and the bar can also be built of balsa. Fasten pocket mirrors on the wall behind the bar. Cram the entire area full of customers. An entertainment bar like Finn's has standing room only! Little details like swinging doors, pictures on the walls, bottles and food on the bar and tables all contribute to make this scene interesting and believable.

Proper lighting adds considerable credibility to a model like Finn's. Six individual dim house lights are suspended from the ceiling in the main room. They are

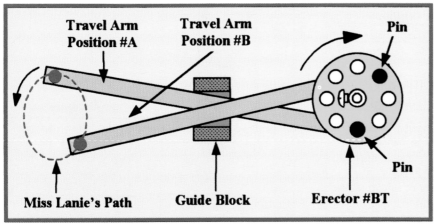

Figure 3   Mechanism Detail showing two travel arm posititons with motor removed (Top View)

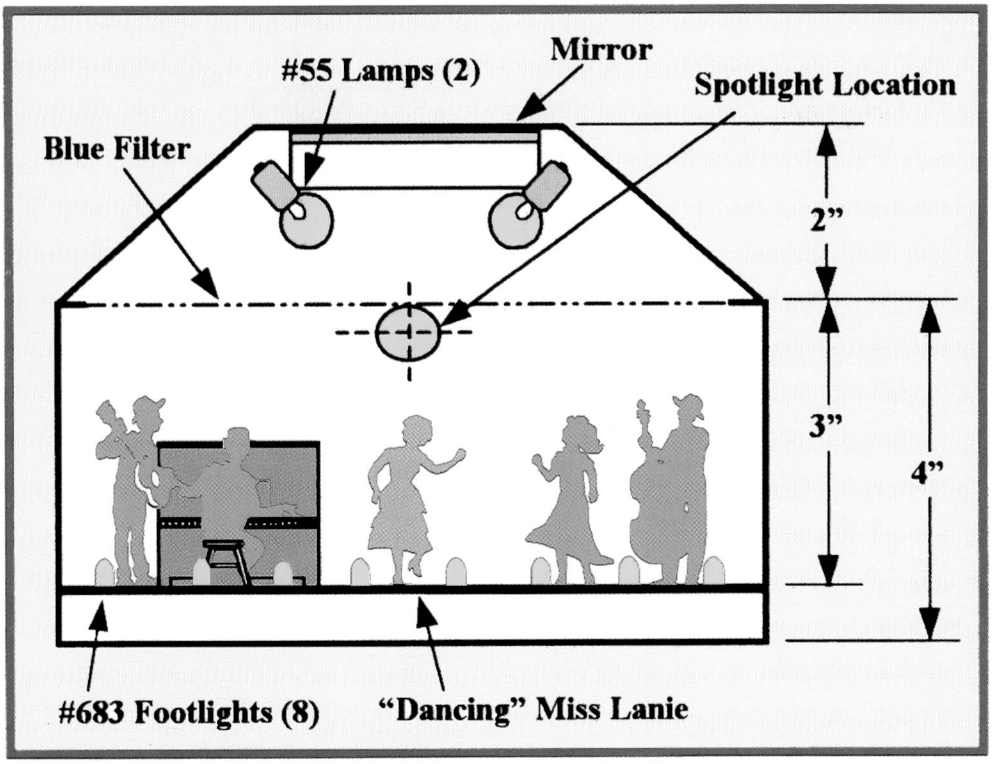

the blue stage. This light should be mounted so Miss Lanie spends at least most of her time in it as she dances around.

A six-pin connector is optionally used so that the building can be easily removed from the layout for adjustment or lamp replacement. (The brighter stage lights are more prone to burn-out that the #683 lamps,) Wiring for the connector is shown in Figure 5. Note that the lamps and motor share a common ground. If this cannot be arranged with your motor, then a separate two-pin connector should be used for its power.

Sound is provided via an auto-reverse cassette player. The Little Lakes Lines saloon uses a tape recording made from the Dunhill record #DS 50009, "Mickey Finn's - America's No. 1 Speakeasy". This particular recording has great saloon songs such as "The Beer Barrel Polka", "Let me Call You Sweetheart", "Bye Bye, Blackbird" and "When the Saints Come Marching In" all played on honky tonk piano with miscellaneous accompanying instruments. In addition, the whole crowd is singing, hooting, hollering, clapping and having a grand old time!

Roof design is not critical other than at least 2" of space above the main room and stage should be available to house the lighting system. Use 3/32" balsa

Figure 4   Finn's Saloon Stage Detail

here too. The roof should be made removable to allow accessibility to the lighting, motor and speakers. Ventilators, blowers and air conditioner units may be added here to increase interest.

made from #683 lamps wired as shown in Figure 5. Then #4 flat washers are glued to the top of the light bulbs to serve as shades as depicted in Figure 2. A pair of #55 large globe lamps are mounted overhead to illuminate the stage area. A piece of blue cellophane is used between these lights and the stage so that a strong blue color is cast upon the entertainers. A pocket mirror mounted in the building's ceiling helps to make the blue lighting more intense and evenly distributed. Miss Lanie is spotlighted by a #44 lamp which is mounted in a position where it can shine directly upon the stage without passing through the blue filter. This lamp is wrapped in a cardboard or electrical tape shroud to form a light-directing cylinder (See Figures 2 and 4). Consequently, a definitive round spot of white light is projected upon

A single #44 lamp is used to illuminate the restaurant wing of the saloon. Here booth-type seating is provided for those seeking a quieter meal. Inclusion of this entire section is completely optional.

Outside, there is a large entrance sign with a border of red LEDs (Light Emitting Diodes) to draw customers to the saloon. There are a total of 70 LEDs connected in parallel. They are powered by 6 volts AC through two 40 ohm resistors connected in series as illustrated in Figure 5. A relay timer is used to place a 10 ohm resistor in parallel with one of the 40 ohm resistors. Although the LED border is always ON, it will glow considerably brighter when the relay is closed. The LED scheme is very device

With the roof of Finn's Saloon removed, you can see the overhead lights above the blue gel. There is a mirror in the roof piece that also reflects the light downward. The dance motor mechanism and speaker can be seen at the right. These are out of sight behind the red curtain.

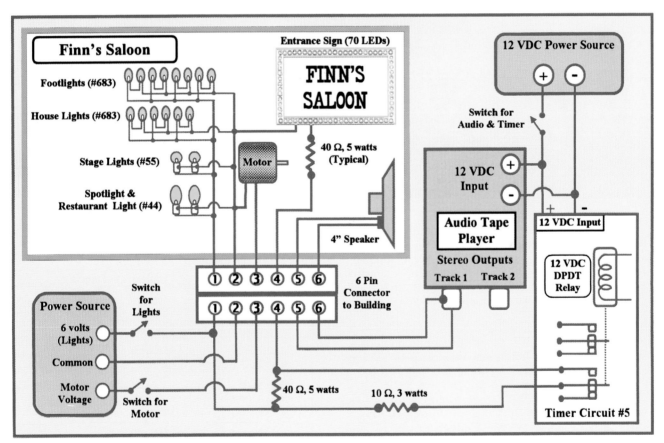

Figure 5 Finn's Saloon Wiring Diagram

dependent. Resistor values here will not necessarily be valid for other types of LEDs, and there are many. Trial and error is probably the best way to determine resistor values for the brightness change that you desire. The intent here is to surface the basic idea of creating a sign with an illuminated border which will periodically vary in brightness to gather attention.

Dry transfer lettering is used on the sign and the building side. The font is 48 point "Quentin". It was selected for its "old time" frilly-style.

The saloon continues to be one of the most intriguing places in Podunk City. Hopefully, customers will soon be beating down the doors to get into your establishment too!

Podunk School of Dance
(This Project uses Electrical Circuit No. 1 and two No. 5 Circuits)

Table 1   School of Dance Parts List

Quan.	Item	Description
3 ea.	Balsa Wood	3" x 3/32" x 36"
5 ea.	Windows	1" x 1 5/8"
4 ea.	Figure	Ballerinas (Dancing)
2 ea.	Figure	Ballerinas (Standing)
9 ea.	Figure	Standing instructor/observers
5 ea.	Figure	Seated observers
6 ea.	Chair	Folding or straight back
4 ea.	Pocket mirrors	2" x 3"
1 ea.	Brass Rod	1/32" x 12"
1 ea.	Motor	60 rpm
1 ea.	Motor	30 rpm
2 ea.	Motor	10 rpm
5 ea.	Lamp	#1445, 18 Volts, .15 A
2 ea.	Power Switch	SPST
1 ea.	Circuit # 1	12 VDC Component Set
2 ea.	Circuit # 5	Component Set
1 ea.	Resistor	220 KΩ, ¼ watt
1 ea.	Resistor	330 KΩ, ¼ watt
2 ea.	Resistor	2.2 MΩ, ¼ watt
2 ea.	Capacitor	10 μf, 16 VDC (Tantalum)

The "Arts" are alive and well in Podunk City. The Podunk School of Dance is located above the Podunk Arts Theater where live stage shows are presented daily. Here graceful ballerinas whirl about as they practice their pirouettes. Hopefully they will earn starring roles in the ballet productions that are periodically held in the theater below. Visitors may peer through the large windows to see the dancers perform a recital. This interesting and unusual scene is a very easy one to model and animate. The dance studio may be located over a theater as in this example; over a block of stores, or as a freestanding structure.

Major parts required for fabrication of the dance school are listed in Table 1. It is constructed entirely of sheet balsa. There are 5 large windows for easy viewing of the detailed interior as may be seen in the Figure 1 floor plan. No exterior doors are indicated as this room is located on the second floor level. The interior door is simply a scrap piece of thin sheet balsa with a small straight pin doorknob.

Mirrored walls with a practice bar are the basic furnishings of ballet dance training rooms. Standard 2" x 3" pocket mirrors may be used on the walls without need for cutting. Figure 2 shows the relative size of a wall with mirrors installed. They form a scale 8' high mirror area in the room that has a 10' ceiling height. (Each mirror segment is a scale 8' high by 12' wide.) A 1/32" brass rod mounted about a scale 3' above the floor serves as the practice bar. Clever positioning of the ballerinas and mirrors can give the on-looker the impression that there are more dancers moving than in reality.

Movement is produced by four motors concealed under the floor as illustrated in Figure 3. The drive shaft of each motor extends just slightly above the top of the

48

Table 2   Circuit References & Electrical Values

Device	Reference	R_A	R_B	C
Motors #1 & #2 Timer	Circuit #5	330 KΩ (¼ watt)	220 KΩ (¼ watt)	10 µf (16 VDC)
Motors #3 & #4 Timer	Circuit #5	2.2 MΩ (¼ watt)	2.2 MΩ (¼ watt)	10 µf (16 VDC)

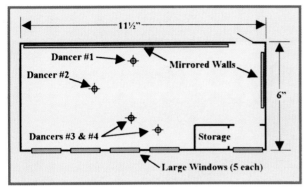

Figure 1   School of Dance Floor Plan

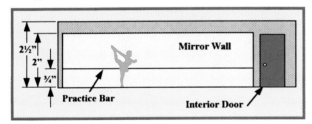

Figure 2   Mirror Wall Detail

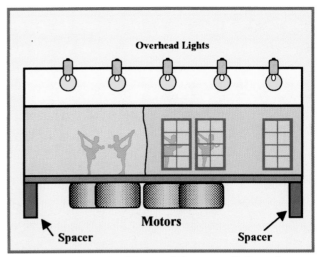

Figure 3   School of Dance "Cut-a-way" Overview

diagram. Motors with three different speed ranges are used. One each turns at 60 and 30 rpm, and two each revolve at 10 rpm. The two low speed dancers are located closest to the windows. They periodically revolve together as a set and do more twirling than resting. One each of the higher speed ballerinas is always turning, but never simultaneously. ON and OFF cycling is controlled by the two relay timer circuits. Five lamps are concealed in the ceiling to evenly illuminate the entire scene.

Elegant and fancy wall decorations may be made from trinkets used to construct bracelets, pins, etc. These are commonly found in craft stores. Chairs should be set about the room for visitors who have arrived to watch the recital. The ballerina figures may be found in stores, which sell crafts, party supplies, and/or cake decorations. Potted plants of lichen or plastic foliage clippings may also be added to beautify the room.

Be sure to check the view through the windows before setting the unit on your layout. The wall of mirrors can be a little tricky. You do not want your visitors to see more than they should. For example, the mirrors allow you to see the wall containing the windows you are looking through. Make sure that you paint and finish this wall so that it matches the quality of the rest of the room! (Normally, without mirrors, you would never see such an area.)

When all is satisfactory, install the entire assembly in your city. Watch the dancers practice and wish them luck on their future auditions! Unfortunately, the ballerinas at the Podunk School of Dance have not quite made the grade yet. Years and years have gone by and the same people are still there practicing!

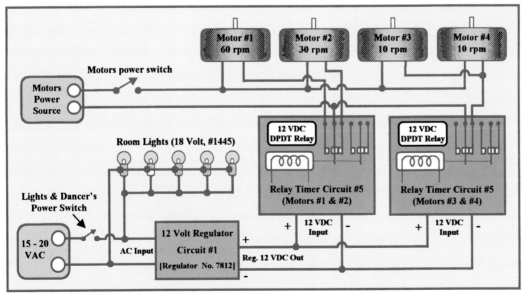

Figure 4   School of Dance Wiring Diagram

finished floor. Model dancers may then be glued directly to each motor shaft. Ballerina figures are most appropriate for this application. Their pirouette dance movement consists of full turns of the body on the point of the toe or the ball of the foot in ballet. It is a great motion to practice and the model dancers will insist on doing it again and again!

Figure 4 shows the motor control scheme and wiring

How can a town on a model railroad layout be complete without a hobby shop? Roy's Hobbies in the center of Podunk City naturally features model trains! The miniature customers are drawn like a magnet to the gorgeous train display in the store window. There is a long Santa Fe freight pulled by a F3 diesel in the stunning war-bonnet paint scheme streaking along the lush foothills of the Rocky Mountains. They gaze intently through the store window as the F3's dazzling headlight sweeps across the display as the train approaches. It soon passes and the rear red end-of-train light can be seen until it disappears into a mountain tunnel. Looking through the shop's doorway, one can see orange and blue boxes everywhere! No wonder there is such a crowd of people inside the store! This building with its illuminated, operating model train in the display window will command the full attention of your full-sized layout visitors as well!

Roy's Hobbies is a balsa wood structure that nestles between Milller's 5¢ & 10¢ Store and the Podunk Arts Center Theater at Podunk City. Major components of the shop are listed in Table 1. Miscellaneous materials including paints, glue, balsa wood scraps, wire, tape, lichen, stones, etc. are needed to complete the scene.

Begin with fabrication of the storefront. This is made separable from the rear section to allow access for interior detailing and the moving train display. It consists of a sheet of 3/32" thick balsa cut as shown in Figure 1. The door is built up of balsa strips to allow for plenty of glass viewing area. A single piece of Plexiglas is placed behind the cutout door and large train display window. The shop's name sign is made of dry transfer lettering on translucent tracing paper. It is affixed to the Plexiglas with transparent tape, out of sight behind solid sections of the structure. Lighting from behind will then effectively illuminate the sign as well as the interior of the shop.

Next the "front-less" store is constructed of sheet

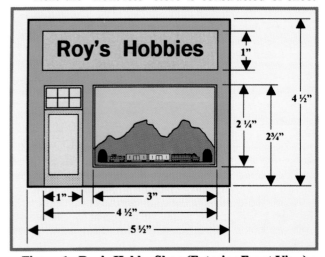

Figure 1   Roy's Hobby Shop (Exterior Front View)

Table 1 Roy's Hobby Shop Parts List

Quan.	Item	Description
7 ea.	"O" Figures	Roy & customers inside shop
1 ea.	Wood base	4"x 5½", ½" Plywood
1 ea.	Motor	10 rpm with ≈1/8" dia. shaft
1 ea.	Pierced Disk	Erector #BT
1 ea.	Glass Paint	Transpaent red
1 ea.	Glue	Balsa wood - normal drying.
2 ea.	Balsa Wood	4" x 5" x 3/32" (Shop sides)
1 ea.	Balsa Wood	5"x 5½"x 3/32" (Shop front)
1 ea.	Balsa Wood	5"x 5½"x 3/32" (Shop back)
1 ea.	Balsa Wood	2¾"x 5½"x ¾" (Motor base)
1 ea.	Balsa Wood	3¼"x 3½"x 3/16" (Backdrop)
1 ea.	Balsa Wood	2½"x 3¼"x 3/16" (Shelf back)
1 ea.	Balsa Wood	¾"x 3/16"x 18" (Counters)
1 ea.	Balsa Wood	¼"x ¼"x 18" (Train, bracing)
1 ea.	Plexiglas	3" circle. (Train base disk)
1 ea.	Plexiglas	4½"x 4¾"x 1/8" (Windows)
1 ea.	Pierced Disk	Erector #BT
1 ea.	Collar	Erector #P37
1 ea.	Brass Tube	≈1/8" O.D. , 6" long (Size to slip over motor shaft)
1 ea.	Heat Shrink	≈1/8" I.D. , 4" long (Insulates 1/8" Tube)
1 ea.	Brass Tube	≈5/32" I.D., 3" long (Slides over heat shrink tube)
1 ea.	Brass Tube	≈3/16" I.D., 1" long (Stationary wiper contact)
1 ea.	Brass Strip	≈¾" x 2" x 1/32" (Support)
4 ea.	Lamps	#57, 12 -16 volt, min. bayonet
4 ea.	Lamp Socket	Miniature bayonet
2 ea.	Lamps	#683, 5 volts, 60 ma.
2 ea.	Machine Screw	8-32, ½"long
2 ea.	Lockwashers	#8
2 ea.	Nut	8-32
2 ea.	Power Switch	SPST

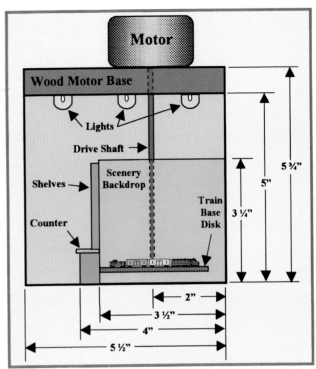

Figure 2 Roy's Hobby Shop (Interior Front View)

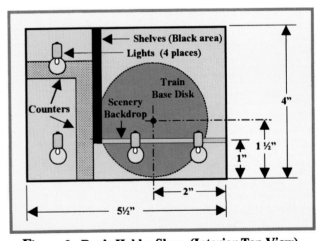

Figure 3 Roy's Hobby Shop (Interior Top View)

balsa mounted on a 1/2" plywood base for rigidity. See Figures 2 and 3. The interior walls of the store may be finished with dollhouse wallpaper scraps and train signs in the customer area. A heavier balsa block is positioned on top of the shop's room to support the motor.

Fabrication techniques used to create the train display are illustrated in Figures 4, 5, and 6. A 10 rpm synchronous motor is ideal for this application. The Plexiglas train base disk is about 3" in diameter. It is painted black. Two, or three, silver rails are then painted on it as shown in Figure 5. Fasten the disk to an Erector #BT pierced disk, or equivalent, with two machine screws.

Build up the electrical contact slip ring/wiper assembly in accordance with Figure 4. Attach it to disk #BT so that the whole assembly appears as shown in the drawing. It can then be connected to the motor shaft via the #P37 collar. This arrangement provides the electrical current paths to illuminate the train lights.

The model train is carved from 1/4" square balsa,

painted and glued to the "track" on the base disk. Carve a notch in the locomotive and caboose to accept the #683 lamps. The two lights are wired in series and connected to the disk and brass contacts as depicted in Figure 4. Color the caboose light with transparent red glass paint. Although obviously not a fine scale model train, some clever painting, the lights, and its quick motion leave no doubt in the viewer's mind as to what it is.

Fit the entire assembly to the store section. The brass support contact helps to steady the revolving disk. Power the motor to test the unit before everything is glued in place around it. The disk should revolve freely. Test the lights to make sure that the slip ring/wiper assembly is making good contact. When all is well, the assembly is affixed by wood screws and/or glue.

Next, the scenic backdrop should be fabricated. It is a simple balsa board with two tunnel entrances. Snow-capped mountains, blue sky, some miniature stones and lichen bushes complete the model scene, See Figure 6. There is a bit of fitting required to bring the scenery as

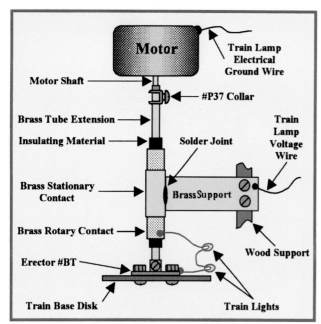

Figure 4   Train Base Disk Mechanism

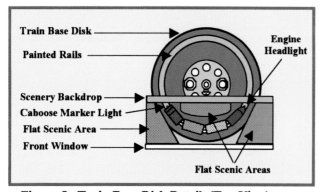

Figure 5   Train Base Disk Detail (Top View)

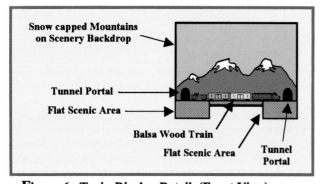

Figure 6   Train Display Detail (Front View)

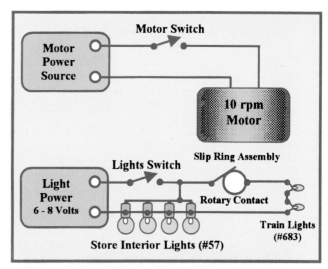

Figure 7   Roy's Hobby Shop Wiring Diagram

Removing the building's front wall (above) reveals the operating mechanism. Most of the animations are built as separate modules (left) which can be removed for service.

close as practical to the smooth running train. The closer it is, the better it looks. The whole unit must be carefully formed to not interfere with the rotating display.

The store shelves and the counters extending towards the rear of the shop may also be made as part of this background assembly. Finish the interior scene by placing painted balsa block "train boxes" on the shelves, some balsa block "trains" on the counter, a salesman behind the counter, and a gaggle of ecstatic customers.

Figure 7 shows the wiring scheme for the hobby shop animation. It would be best to power the lights at about 6 to 8 volts. This will result in a more realistic level of illumination. The #57 lamps have relatively

large globes which provide for quite an even dispersion of light throughout the store's interior.

Upon setting the shop on your layout, don't forget to place a large crowd of people outside the train display window. Some will undoubtedly have their noses pressed hard against the glass! This may well become the most popular establishment in your town!

Chapter Six

The country category encompasses a wide variety of scenic settings. Mountains, gently rolling foothills, farmlands, brooks, rivers, bays, and even the ocean all come to mind. Consequently, country-oriented scenes are very diverse and open up an almost limitless number of interesting animation possibilities. The examples are so widely varied, it soon becomes evident that this is but the tip of the iceberg. The broad range of scenes that one may pursue to create becomes nothing short of amazing! The following Little Lakes Lines country-oriented scene scenarios are presented in this chapter.

Perched on a high mountain hillside, a group of teenagers are flying a tethered model airplane. As the plane changes its flight-path and altitude, the roar of its engine fluctuates in precise synchronism with the changing speed. Deep in the river valley, a group of children are happily flying a kite that darts up and down along the Rocky River bank. Downstream, a bulldozer is hard at work. It shakes and rumbles as it attempts to position heavy boulders to halt erosion that is threatening a nearby railroad bridge. Warning beacons wink on a fixed span railroad bridge by the ocean inlet harbor to warn boatmen of its low clearance and of the treacherous rapids that lie just beyond. Along a country road, oncoming automobiles wink their headlights in warning to approaching motorists. Yes, there is a speed trap ahead with a motorcycle-mounted trooper quietly waiting behind a gigantic lichen bush! Country and cows go together. Here we have the Poppa Cow Dairy building with men constantly transferring milk cans. Farmers from the "Bar F" Ranch daily bring their fresh milk to be loaded onto the Little lakes Lines reefers for their journey to the cities and towns. Mentioning "country" also reminds one of live acoustic country music. To this end, the LLL inhabitants hop a train each Saturday night and head for Albert Music Hall. Albert Music Hall is a place where acoustic musicians gather weekly to play their country, bluegrass, and folk songs. This building, patterned after the prototype in Waretown, NJ, provides a real sight and sound feast for the eyes and ears.

Most all of the foregoing scenarios are quite simple to model. Furthermore, the basic ideas and techniques can be readily and easily custom-tailored to your preferences for use on your layout.

Model Airplane
(This Project uses Electrical Circuit No. 1 and three No. 5 Circuits)

Flying model airplanes is a great way to spend an afternoon. These children have climbed to a high flat field on Mole Hill. Here they fly their remote controlled tethered aircraft. The roar of the model's engine can be heard as the airplane turns, dives, and swoops. Engine noise softens as the plane glides along, then increases as power is applied, culminating in a mighty roar as the plane's throttle is fully opened. An exciting sight indeed! Build this scene for your layout and your visitors will not believe their eyes and ears!

Implementation of this scene requires a bit of forethought. First, the scene is most effectual if located high and somewhat in the background. This is strongly recommended, as a two to three inch diameter opening in the "ground" is required to accommodate the wildly moving airplane's support wire "tether". Consequently, a figure cannot be placed sufficiently close to the wire to convince anyone that he or she is really operating the airplane. By locating the animation in a high remote location, bushes and trees can be employed to disguise the hole and the absence of a miniature operator from the onlooker's line of sight. Thus attention is directed only to the flying aircraft. Second, about a foot of space directly below the tether's "ground" level exit hole, and reasonable access to it, is required for placement of the operating mechanism. The Little Lakes Line's large hollow plaster-on-screen mountains are ideal for this purpose.

Figures 1 and 2 illustrate the mechanical drive configuration that animates the airplane. There are two motors. One is designated as the "Fly" Motor and the other as the "Tilt" Motor. The "Fly" Motor simply rotates the plane in a circle. Speed of rotation is randomly varied by relay control as either "low", "medium", or "high". Correspondingly, these same relays also provide accompanying "low", "medium", or "high" motor roar sound. The "Tilt" Motor moves the angle-arm girder upon which the "Fly" Motor is mounted. Power is periodically applied to this motor in short pulses causing it to move a little and then stop. Every stop position is random and directly effects both the altitude of the airplane and the angle at which it is flying. Each stop position results in a different altitude and angle of flight. The miniature plane may be constructed of carved balsa wood as shown in Figure 3. Paint it bright so that it will be easy to follow in flight. It is necessarily quite tiny as it is but a model used by your miniature people! A one-inch long wingspan equates to 4' in scale!

Table 1 Model Airplane Parts List

Quan.	Item	Description
-	"O" Figures	Children to "Fly" the Plane.
1 ea.	Balsa Wood	3/16" x 3/16" x 12" (Airplane Body)
1 ea.	Balsa Wood	1/8" x 1/16" x 12" (Airplane Wings)
1 ea.	Balsa Wood	¼" x 1/32" x 12" (Airplane Vertical Tail)
1 ea.	Balsa Wood	1/8" x 1/32" x 12" (Airplane Tail Wings)
-	Acrylic Paint	Bright Airplane Colors
1 ea.	Spring Steel Wire	≈ 1/32" Diameter, 24" Long
1 ea.	Collar	Erector #P37 (Wire Clamp)
1 ea.	6" Angle Girder	Erector #BE "Fly" Motor Mount Arm
1 ea.	11 Hole Strip	Erector #H
1 ea.	Pierced Disk	Erector #BT
2 ea.	Machine Screw	6-32 x 1" Long
2 ea.	Lockwashers	#6
6 ea.	Nuts	6-32
4 ea.	Flat Washers	#6 Hole, 1" Diameter
1 ea.	Mounting Base	Wood, Approx. 4" x 8"

Table 2 Model Airplane Electrical Parts List

Quan.	Item	Description
3 ea.	Power Switch	SPST
2 ea.	*Motors, 12 VDC	≈ 0 – 200 rpm
2 ea.	Bridge Rectifier	1.4 Amp., 100 PIV
1 ea.	Circuit # 1	12 VDC Component Set
3 ea.	Circuit # 5	Component Set
2 ea.	Capacitor	.047 µf, 50 volt
2 ea.	Capacitor	2.2 µf, 16 VDC (Tantalum)
1 ea.	Capacitor	22 µf, 16 VDC (Tantalum)
1 ea.	Resistor	82 KΩ, ¼ watt
1 ea.	Resistor	330 KΩ, ¼ watt
2 ea.	Resistor	390 KΩ, ¼ watt
2 ea.	Resistor	820 KΩ, ¼ watt
1 ea.	*Resistor, Power	≈ 10Ω, 10 watts "Tilt" Motor Limiter
1 ea.	*Resistor, Power	≈ 10Ω, 10 watts "Fly" Motor Limiter
1 ea.	*Resistor, Power	≈ 7Ω, 10 watts "Fly" Motor – Low Speed
1 ea.	*Resistor, Power	≈ 3Ω, 10 watts "Fly" Motor – Medium Speed
1 ea.	*Resistor, Power	≈ 5Ω, 10 watts Audio – Low Volume
1 ea.	*Resistor	≈ 2Ω, 10 watts Audio – Medium Volume
1 ea.	4" Speaker	8Ω, 4 watts or higher
1 ea.	Tape Player	Auto-Reverse or 3 minute Endless Loop cassette.

* Note: Motor & resistor characteristics are interdependent. These are the resistor values used with the motors utilized by the Little Lakes Lines.

Parts required for assembly of the model plane animation are identified in Tables 1 and 2. A word about the motors. These are 12 volt DC permanent magnet motors. There are many types, such as those used in scale model railroads, which may be used. Shaft speed should range from zero to a couple hundred revolutions per minute (rpm). Motors specified as rotating in the thousands of rpm will require a gearbox to reduce their speed. Some motors, like the ones used on the Little Lakes Lines came with a gearbox in place. Where Erector Set parts are identified; brass or similar metal pieces may be readily substituted.

The Model Airplane Wiring Diagram is presented in Figure 4. This complex-appearing drawing consists of three completely separate operational elements: (1) the timer control circuits, (2) the motor control circuits, and (3) the sound control circuits. Each element is shown with its own power supply and power switch. Power supplies may be shared if common voltage

Table 3 Circuit References & Electrical Values

Device	Reference	R_A	R_B	C
"Fly" Motor Timer #A	Circuit #5	820 KΩ (¼ watt)	330 KΩ (¼ watt)	22 µf (16 VDC)
"Fly" Motor Timer #B	Circuit #5	390 KΩ (¼ watt)	390 KΩ (¼ watt)	2.2 µf (16 VDC)
"Tilt" Motor Timer #C	Circuit #5	820 KΩ (¼ watt)	82 KΩ (¼ watt)	2.2 µf (16 VDC)

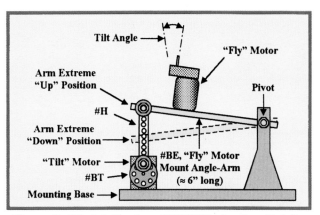

Figure 2 Model Airplane "Tilt" Mechanism Detail

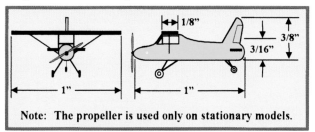

Note: The propeller is used only on stationary models.

Figure 3 Model Airplane Detail

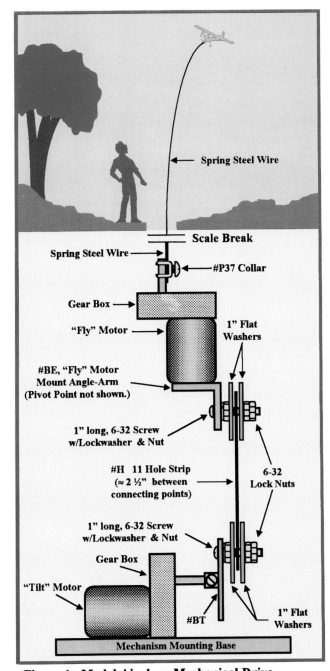

Figure 1 Model Airplane Mechanical Drive

requirements should exist between multiple elements, and "OFF-ON" functions combined to a single multi-pole switch.

Element 1 - Timer control circuits. A single 15-20 VAC power source, "OFF-ON" switch, and 12 VDC Regular Circuit (Circuit #1) support the three identical Relay Timers (Circuit #5). The resistor and capacitor values for each timer are delineated in Table 3. The timer control circuits are electrically isolated from the other elements, which are controlled solely through relay contacts.

Element 2 - Motor control circuits. Motor control depends entirely upon the individual characteristics of the selected motors. A 6 VAC power supply is used by the LLL. The independently controlled "Tilt" and the "Fly" Motors are treated identically because they have the same electrical/mechanical characteristics. As these are DC motors powered by an AC source, each is shown connected to a bridge rectifier (AC/DC conversion) and a capacitor for spike suppression.

The "Tilt" Motor is activated through Timer #C relay contacts. This timer is set to provide periodic short bursts of power to the motor. Motor speed is determined via the power source voltage and the value of the "Tilt" Motor "Limiter" resistor. It should be set so that the motor shaft moves just a fraction of a turn when pulsed. Increasing the value of this resistor will slow the motor, while decreasing its value will have the opposite effect.

The fastest rotating speed of the "Fly" Motor is determined by the value of the "Fly" Motor "Limiter" resistor. Set this value to produce the quickest rotational speed desired for your airplane. Again, increasing the resistor's value will slow the airplane and decreasing it will cause it to speed up. Energizing Relay #A will cause the plane to travel at top speed. It will fly at medium speed when Relay #B is active as determined by the value of the "Fly" Motor medium speed resistor. When neither relay is active, the plane will move slowest as set by the "Fly" Motor low speed resistor.

Element 3 - Sound control circuits. Motor noise is played from a tape player through a speaker located near the animation. A surprisingly good airplane-like sound may be achieved by recording the sound of a common portable power drill! Make the recording with a single volume setting to produce a sustained high

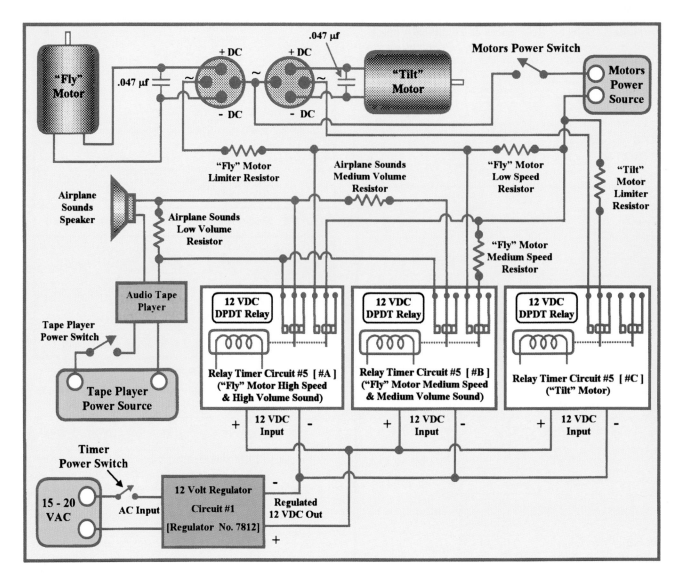

level tone.

Make a test volume level setting by playing the completed tape in the animation's Tape Player with it's output connected directly to the speaker. When so arranged, turn the player's volume control to produce the loudest desired tone. It should remain at this setting for use with the animation. This highest sound level will be heard when Relay #A is activated. A medium level of sound is determined by the value of the "Airplane Sounds Medium Volume Resistor" shown in Figure 4 and is played when Relay #B is turned ON. Similarly, the lowest level of sound is set by the value of "Airplane Sounds Low Volume Resistor" and is heard when neither relay is active. Controlling both speaker output levels and "Fly" Motor speeds by the same relays ensures that motor noise intensity and aircraft rotational speed are always in perfect synchronization.

When the mechanism and speaker system have proven to operate properly on the bench, proceed to install them on the layout. Carefully place trees and bushes to conceal the exit hole of the spring steel tether. A group of children should be placed in the vicinity to suggest to the viewer that someone is actually operating the controls. They should have numerous model airplanes, painted in a wide variety of colors in their possession, as they anxiously wait their turn to fly. Heighten scene interest by including a model plane stuck in a nearby tree and/or one that has crashed into a pile of rubble on the ground! Anyone who has flown model planes can really relate to heart-stopping mishaps such as these. It really makes one appreciate the durability and longevity of model trains.

56

Bulldozer
(This Project uses Electrical Circuits No. 1 and No. 6)

Bulldozers may be seen most anywhere along a railroad's right-of-way. The Little Lakes Lines has one working by a sharp turn in the Rocky River. The road crew is placing heavy boulders along this particular section to help retain the riverbank when spring rains swell it to near flood stage.

The bulldozer makes a most interesting animation, as its actions are both compound and somewhat unpredictable. Action is compounded in the sense that the machine has a horrendous vibration as it works its way over the rocky terrain. It is like a high speed "shake". Simultaneously, it is slowly moving back and forth attempting to push huge boulders into position. An intentionally loose mechanical link between the bulldozer and the drive crank mechanism results in constant changes of direction with each succeeding push and reverse cycle.

Figure 1 shows the Little Lakes Lines mechanical configuration of this animation. Parts are listed in Tables 1 and 2. About a foot of space beneath the tabletop is required for the drive mechanism. The illustrated implementation makes extensive use of numerous Erector Set components. Alternatively, these parts may be fabricated from brass rods, strips, and wood pieces.

Construction begins with mounting the crank at the table top bulldozer site. A good bearing surface is a necessity. It may be provided by first drilling a generous size clearance hole through the table. The actual bearing surfaces are then formed by attaching metal strips (e.g. Erector # F) with wood screws on either side of the table top as shown in Figure 1. The crank's vertical position is held by a metal collar (e.g. Erector # P37) with a spacer washer to assure that the setscrew clears the heads of the screws holding the bearing strip. A hori-

Table 1 Bulldozer Parts List

Quan.	Item	Description
1 ea.	Bulldozer	"O" Gauge Metal model
1 ea.	Motor	12 VDC, ≈7 RPM
1 ea.	Motor	12 VDC, ≈100 RPM
1 ea.	Circuit #1	12 VDC Component Set
1 ea.	Circuit #6	Component Set
1 ea	Resistor	2.2 MΩ (¼ watt)
1 ea.	Capacitor	47 μf (16 VDC)
2 ea.	Pierced Disk	Erector #BT
3 ea.	Metal Strip	Erector #F (≈1½" long)
1 ea.	Metal Strip	Erector #H (≈3" long)
1 ea.	Metal Strip	Erector #I (≈5½" long)
1 ea.	Motor Carrier	See Table 2 for part list.
5 ea.	Collar	Erector #P37
1 ea.	Eccentric Crank	Erector #AA (or #BT)
1 ea.	Axle Rod	Erector: ≈4" long
1 ea.	Crank	Erector #P24
4 ea.	Wood Screw	No. 8, ½" long
2 ea.	Machine Screw	8-32, ½" long
4 ea.	Machine Screw	8-32, 1" long
9 ea.	Nut	8-32
6 ea.	Lockwasher	No. 8
1 ea.	Power Switch	SPST

Table 2 Motor Carrier Frame Parts List
(Erector Part Implementation)

Quan.	Item	Description
2 ea.	Base Plate	Erector #MC
1 ea.	Angle Girder	Erector #BE (6" long)
1 ea.	Girder	Erector #B
1 ea.	Flat Plate	Erector #MF
10 ea.	Machine Screw	8-32, ½" long
10 ea.	Nut	8-32
10 ea.	Lockwasher	No. 8

Table 3 Circuit Reference & Electrical Values

Device	Reference	R	C
Relay Timer	Circuit #6	2.2 MΩ (¼ watt)	47 µf (16 VDC)

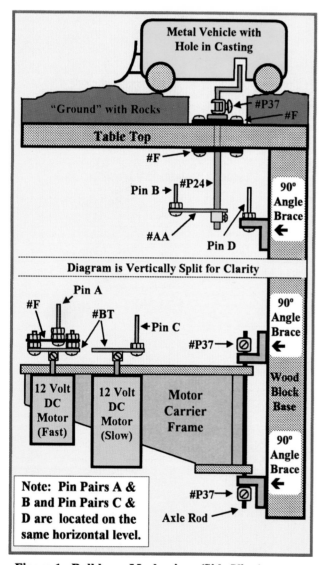

Note: Pin Pairs A & B and Pin Pairs C & D are located on the same horizontal level.

Figure 1 Bulldozer Mechanism (Side View)

zontal eccentric crank (e.g. Erector # AA) is attached to the lower part of the crank rod. This is a good time to place your metal vehicle on the crank "handle" while supported by your finished rocky roadbed. Most metal

vehicles have some sort of underside hole available that would suit this purpose. If not, it will be necessary to drill an oversized hole in the bottom of the bulldozer. When complete, wigwag the eccentric crank back & forth by hand to make sure that the bulldozer moves as expected. Its motion will depend largely on the terrain upon which it is situated.

A "Motor Carrier Frame" can be constructed as shown in Figures 1, 2 and 3 to provide the desired compound motion. Mount the two motors on the frame in accordance with the illustrations. It is advisable that lockwashers be installed under all nuts as the considerable vibration forces will tend to loosen the fasteners over time.

Install a vertical wood block base within about 1" of the crank assembly for mounting the motor carrier frame and the 90° angle brace supporting stationary Pin D. The pins are 1" long #8 machine screws. Place the short slow speed motor linkage over Pin C and Pin D. The turning disk linkage will work against the wood block base thereby causing the motor carrier frame assembly to slowly swing back and forth. The degree of movement is governed by the distance that Pin C is off-center, (1/2"), from the slow motor's shaft. Put the long high speed motor linkage over Pin A and Pin B. This linkage will cause the bulldozer to shift back and forth as the motor carrier frame assembly is moved by the slow motor system. Pin A on the rapidly rotating disk will cause the entire linkage arm, and thereby the bulldozer, to vibrate at the rate of the fast motor's speed. Note that

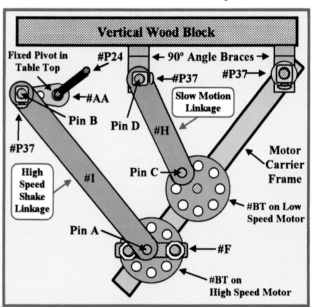

Figure 2 Bulldozer Mechanism

Pin A is located very slightly off-center, (3/16"), from the fast motor's shaft.

A control scheme for the bulldozer animation is shown in Figure 4. The main power switch is optional. It is provided if you should wish to cut off power to the electronic regulator circuit. Actual bulldozer operation is started by the momentary push of a button and is timed to continue for about a minute or so before it automatically turns off. See Table 3 for timer component values. Continuous operation of the bulldozer is not recommended as it is somewhat noisy and could also suffer excessive wearing of certain parts due to its high

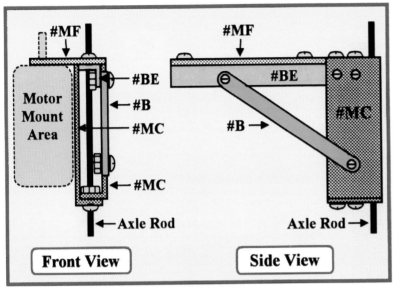

Figure 3   Motor Carrier Frame Detail
(Erector Part Implementation)

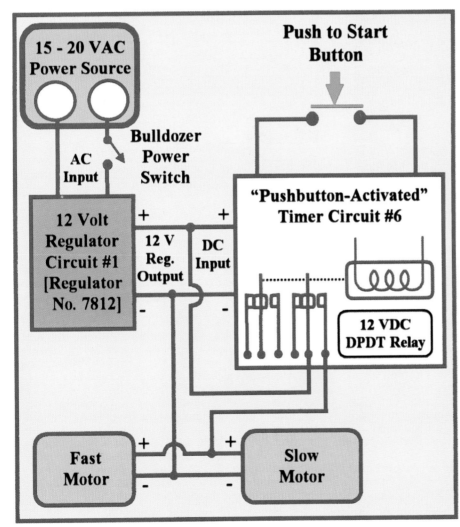

Figure 4 Bulldozer Wiring Diagram

speed action. The two motors are controlled via the timed relay and may be powered from the regulated 12 volt source. Should your motors draw excessive current (i.e. greater than .8 Amp) then they must be connected to an independent power source.

Some final adjustments may be required to fine-tune the operation of your bulldozer. Mechanical positioning for the bulldozer consists of changing the length of the two linkage arms (Erector # H and I). Extent of motion adjustments involve altering the distance of the drive wheel pin location from that of the motor shaft center. The greater the distance, the greater the resulting motion. Lastly, the speed of the motors may be reduced by decreasing the voltage to them. This can be readily accomplished by inserting a small low resistance (10 to 100) power resistor in series with the motor in a trial and error fashion.

Use some rocks around the bulldozer to conceal the crank assembly. Once properly set up, the shaky, push bulldozer is a fascinating thing to watch. Be sure to put a miniature figure in the driver's seat and make sure the seat belt is fastened. It's a rough and tumble ride!

Table 1   Flying Kite Parts List

Quan.	Item	Description
1 ea.	Figure	Figure with raised arm
1 ea.	Kite	Cardstock, balsa & wire
1 ea.	Motor	2 rpm with ≈1/8" dia. shaft
1 ea.	Spring Steel	≈1/32" Diameter, 36" long
1 ea.	Brass Tube	≈3/16"" Diameter, 6" long
1 ea.	"U" Bracket	1/2" copper tube bracket
2 ea.	Wood Screw	No. 8, 3/4" long
1 ea.	Pierced Disk	Erector #BT
1 ea.	Metal Strip	Flat, ≈5" long. (Erector #I)
1 ea.	Sheave Pulley	Erector #AQ
2 ea.	Machine Screw	8-32, ½" long
1 ea.	Machine Screw	8-32, 1" long
4 ea.	Nut	8-32
3 ea.	Lockwasher	No. 8
2	Washers	No. 8
1 ea.	Power Switch	SPST

It's a beautiful balmy day and all the kids' head down to the riverside to fly their kite! This can become a nice action scene on your layout. The kite will glide up as it catches the wind, then slow to a pause. A down-draft will send it on its way towards the earth. It slows again to a brief pause when it catches another breeze and begins to ascend once more. The kite "string" is made of spring steel wire. This material lends a natural sway to the flying kite to suggest that it really is blowing in the wind. A motor, a switch, a kid and a kite is about all you need to build this simple but effective animation!

Figure 1 shows the general configuration of the fly-ing kite mechanism. A tabletop mounting with about two feet of clear space beneath the surface is required. Parts for the flying kite animation are outlined in Table 1.

A 3/16" hole is first drilled in the selected location on the tabletop. A brass tube, about 6" long is inserted. This will form the bearing surface for the spring steel wire. One way to retain the tube in position is to solder it to a standard "U" shaped copper pipe bracket, (made for 1/2" copper tubing) as can be seen in Figures 1 and 2. Attach the bracket to a wood base support using wood screws.

Motor speed should run about 2 rpm. The motor may be attached to a second wood base support as illustrated in the drawing. Standard Erector Set parts are identified in the table and drawings for the project. Other materials could be easily substituted if desired. In any event, the design should be such that the center of the sheave pulley is centered directly under the tube when in the position shown in Figure 2. The sheave pulley acts as a bearing for the spring steel wire. The wire is merely mechanically crimped around the pulley. Spring wire is quite stiff, so make sure it is fastened to the pulley in such a manner that it will remain attached when the pulley is pulling on or pushing against it. A steel machine screw firmly attached via a lockwasher and nut to the drive arm, serves as an axle for the sheave pulley. Loose flat washers are spacers on either side of the sheave pulley to assure that it may freely turn. A pair of "jammed" nuts retains both the washers and pulley on the machine screw axle.

When the motor and drive arm assembly are mounted, thread the spring steel wire through the brass tubing bearing. The wire may extend at any length you deem reasonable above the layout. Children on the Little Lakes Lines fly their kite at about

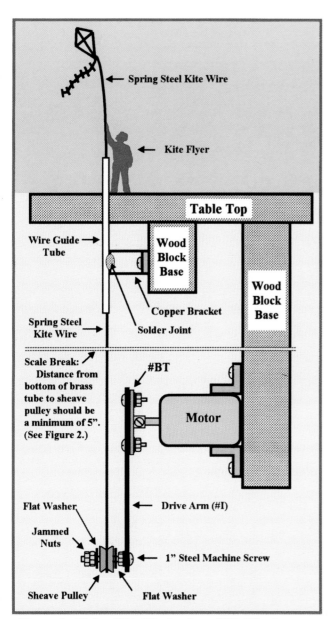

Figure 1 Flying Kite Mechanism (Side View)

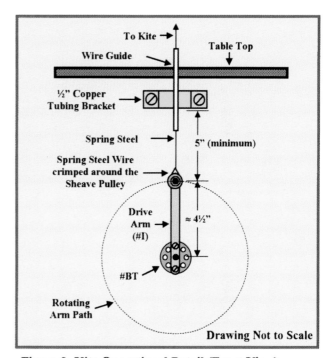

Figure 2 Kite Operational Detail (Front View)

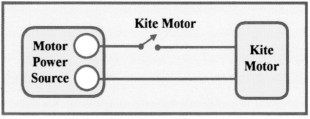

Figure 3 Flying Kite Wiring Diagram

16"-25" above ground level. The change in kite altitude is equal to the diameter of the sheave pulley path during rotation of the drive arm. As may be seen in Figure 2, this distance will be approximately 9".

Building the kite itself is the final step. It consists of a piece of cardstock cut into the shape of a kite. Small scraps of balsa wood are used for the cross members. A short length of bare #22 solid wire, with small pieces of paper glued to it, is used for the tail. Finish the kite by painting as desired and then glue the assembly to the end of the steel wire.

Observe the path that the kite string takes near the ground as you test run the mechanism. Place a figure, preferably a child, with a raised arm in the vicinity of the kite string. Locate the figure to best conceal the guide tube from normal viewing angles. The tube should be judiciously painted to blend in with the surroundings. The steel wire may be left natural or painted to better resemble the kite's cord.

Figure 3 illustrates the wiring for the kite scene as implemented on the Little Lakes Lines. A toggle switch is sufficient as this animation is not wear intensive, and lends itself to continuous operation. The children on your layout should enjoy many happy hours of flying their kite over the trains!

Railroad Bridge Safety Lights
(This Project uses Electrical Circuit No. 3)

Real railroads are forever concerned with safety. The trains have their trackside signals and all highway crossings are well protected with gates and flashing signals. One situation, however, is often overlooked. This involves bridge safety. Low railroad bridges must be appropriately marked so that boats don't go crashing into them. Such a bridge exists near the harbor area on the Little Lakes Lines. The problem is easily solved by the addition of four miniature red warning lights positioned beneath the bridge structure.

To better capture the attention of passing boaters, the center two lights briefly dim at regular intervals while the outer lights remain constant. The warning lights are easy to build and add a bit of interest to an otherwise quite stationary scene. The parts for the warning light project are listed in Tables 1 and 2. Figure 1 details a method of light assembly to restrict excessive glow from the lamps. It also serves to give the impression that the lamps are smaller than they actually are. Two sizes of heat shrink tubing are used in the process. The 3/64" size tubing provides electrical insulation and the subsequent 1/8" size tubing strengthens the leads and provides for excess light shielding. A heat gun or hair dryer may be used to tighten the tubing to the lamp. If neither is available, a spot of glue would also hold things in place. The bulb end can then be dipped into the transparent red glass paint. More than one dipping can be done to obtain a deeper red.

Connect the lamps in accordance with the Figure 2 wiring diagram. This circuit may be wired directly to a 6 volt tap on your transformer. Voltage regulation is

Table 1 Railroad Bridge Safety Lights Parts List

Quan.	Item	Description
4 ea.	Lamps	#683, 5 Volts, 60 ma.
1 ea.	Heat Shrink Tube	3/64" diameter; ≈ 6" length
1 ea.	Heat Shrink Tube	1/8" diameter; ≈ 6" length
1 ea.	Bridge Rectifier	1.4 A, 100 PIV
4 ea.	Diode	1N4001, 50 PIV, 1 Amp
1 ea.	Capacitor	220 µf, 35 VDC
1 ea.	Resistor	22 Ω, ½ watt
1 ea.	Glass Paint	Transparent red
1 ea.	Circuit # 3	Component Set
1 ea.	Resistor	330 KΩ, ¼ watt
1 ea.	Resistor	820 KΩ, ¼ watt
1 ea.	Capacitor	10 µf, 16 VDC (Tantalum)

Table 2 Circuit References & Electrical Values

Device	Reference	R_A	R_B	C
Lamp Timer	Circuit #3	820 KΩ (¼ watt)	330 KΩ (¼ watt)	10 µf (16 VDC)

not necessary as long as a constant 6 volt transformer power supply is available. If not, the 5 volt regulator version of Circuit #1 could be used to facilitate operation at any voltage source from 6 to 25 VAC.

There is no need for a power OFF/ON switch for these lights. They should be continuously operated to

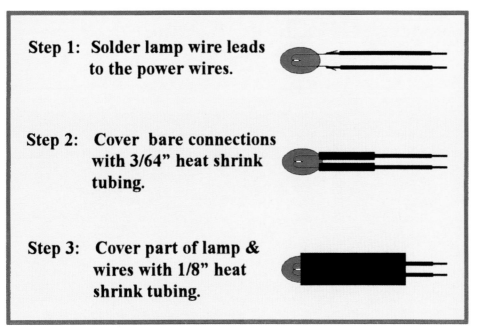

Step 1: Solder lamp wire leads to the power wires.

Step 2: Cover bare connections with 3/64" heat shrink tubing.

Step 3: Cover part of lamp & wires with 1/8" heat shrink tubing.

Figure 1   Light Masking Detail

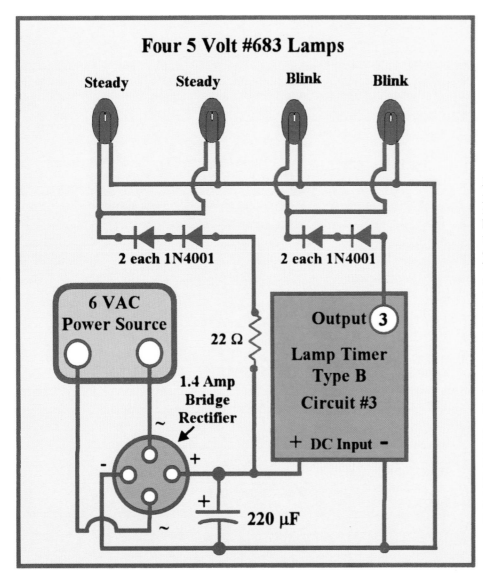

Four 5 Volt #683 Lamps

Steady   Steady   Blink   Blink

2 each 1N4001   2 each 1N4001

6 VAC Power Source

22 Ω

Output ③

Lamp Timer Type B Circuit #3

+ DC Input −

1.4 Amp Bridge Rectifier

~   +   −   ~   +

220 µF

keep your boaters protected! A pair of 1N4001 diodes is connected in both the steady and blinking lamp circuits to soften their brightness, as you will be directly viewing these lamps. The 22 ohm resistor in the steady light circuit helps to keep the steady light pair balanced at the same relative brightness level as the blinking pair. Test the circuitry on the bench first to make sure the light intensity symmetry is acceptable. If not, replace the 22 ohm resistor with one of slightly lesser or greater value.

When all is satisfactory, install them under the span of a bridge on your layout. Your boaters will never have to worry about hitting their heads on bridge girders again and your railroad's lawyers will sleep a little better at night!

Figure 2 Bridge Safety Light Wiring Diagram

Speed Trap Headlight Warning

(This Project uses Electrical Circuits No. 1, No. 2 and No. 5

Ever go a little too fast down the highway when an approaching car gives you two winks of the headlights? Time to slow it down. Must be a speed trap ahead. You travel a little farther and sure enough, there's a motorcycle policeman lurking behind a bush! Now this little scene can be easily reproduced on your layout. Your full-sized visitors will enjoy watching your miniature motorists elude the authorities!

All you need on the layout are two automobiles, a short stretch of road, and some bushes or maybe a billboard where a police car or motorcycle can lurk. Then place the car with the warning headlights a little down the road past the speed trap. An oncoming car is then placed on the roadway facing the first. This car may be fitted with constantly "on" headlights to enhance the scene.

Table 1 lists the parts required to build this scene. The first step is to install the "headlights". This may be done by drilling out the two headlight holes in a vehicle and then inserting a #683 lamp in each. It is a good idea to place a short piece of heat shrink tubing over each lamp to block all light except for the very front of the lens. This is especially important if you have selected a plastic car that would glow unrealistically from any extraneous light. The lamps should then be epoxied in place. Next wire the lamps in series as shown in Figure 1. Attach long wire leads to the lamps wire terminals to facilitate later connection to the electronic control and power circuits.

Specific values for the application dependent components for Timer Circuits #2 and #5 are delineated in Table 2. Circuits #1, #2, and #5 should now be constructed and connected together as shown in Figure 1. The two 150 resistors and two 1N4001 diodes may be mounted together on a small piece of perforated board. They could alternatively be mounted on an unused area of Circuit # 1 or Circuit #5 mounting boards.

When complete, the circuit should operate as follows once the power switch is closed: The headlights

immediately light in a somewhat dim steady level due to the 150 resistor network and 1N4001 diode in the (-) path to the regulated power source. Relay Timer #5 is normally OFF so that path to (-) via the second 1N4001 diode is disconnected by the relay contacts. Meanwhile Timer #2 is continually free-running to provide an alternating electrical (-) and (+) 12 volts at its output. The output OFF/ON rate is that of the "blink-blink" rate of the flashing headlights. However, this output will con-

Table 1   Speed Trap Scene Parts List

Quan.	Item	Description
2 ea.	Cars and/or trucks	One model which allows access to install headlights.
2 ea.	Lamps	#683, 5 Volts, 60 ma.
12"	Tubing	1/8" Heat Shrink
1 ea.	Police car or motorcycle.	Someone to operate the speed trap.
1 ea.	Bush or billboard.	Something to conceal the speed trap.
1 ea.	Circuit # 1	12 VDC Component Set
1 ea.	Circuit # 2	Component Set
1 ea.	Circuit # 5	Component Set
2 ea.	Diodes	1N4001, 50 PIV, 1 Amp
2 ea.	Resistors	150 Ω, ¼ watt
1 ea.	Resistors	150 KΩ, ¼ watt
1 ea.	Resistor	330 KΩ, ¼ watt
1 ea.	Resistor	390 KΩ, ¼ watt
1 ea.	Resistor	1 MΩ, ¼ watt
1 ea.	Capacitor	2.2 μf, 16 VDC (Tantalum)
1 ea.	Capacitor	10 μf, 16 VDC (Tantalum)
1 ea.	Power Switch	SPST

Table 2   Circuit References & Electrical Values

Device	Reference	R_A	R_B	C
Lamp Timer	Circuit #2	330 KΩ (¼ watt)	150 KΩ (¼ watt)	2.2 µf (16 VDC)
Relay Timer	Circuit #5	1 MΩ (¼ watt)	390 KΩ (¼ watt)	10 µf (16 VDC)

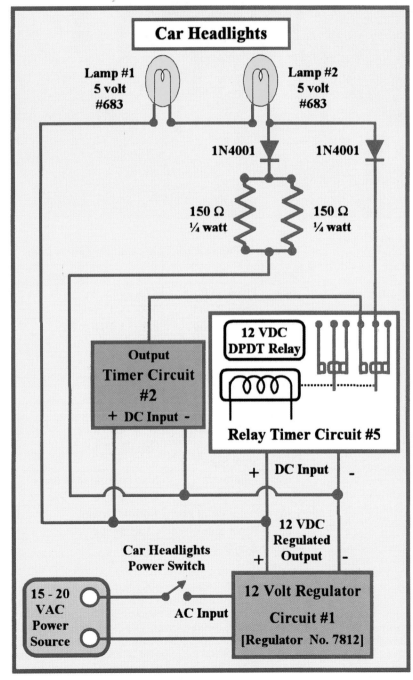

Figure 1   Speed Trap Wiring Diagram

nect to the headlights only when the relay is energized. Relay Timer Circuit #5 is set to be OFF for a duration of many seconds. It's ON time is just long enough to hold the relay contacts closed to allow the (-) output of Timer #2 to be connected to the headlights for two headlight blink periods. This hard (-) connection bypasses the two resistor network that makes the headlights shine brightly for high beam blinking. In Figure 1, the diode pointing to the relay contact prevents the (+) portion of the Timer #2 output from feeding back through the resistors.

Check the completed circuitry on the bench to make sure it operates as expected. If OK, then proceed to install the scene on your layout.

Now you can be certain that at least one of your model cars will not get a speeding ticket today. There should be no wailing sirens on your layout for a while.

Poppa-Cow Dairy
(This Project uses Electrical Circuits No. 1 and No. 5

Located trackside, just a tad down from the Podunk City yard throat, is the renowned Poppa-Cow Dairy. Here recently iced refrigerator cars are loaded with containers of fresh milk. Green pickup trucks from the "Bar F" Ranch continuously deliver full milk cans and then take the empties back to the farm for reuse. A man in the trackside building busily moves milk cans between the truck and the building. A constantly rotating conveyor within the building positions the cans for subsequent transfer to the awaiting refrigerator cars. While this automation is interesting to watch, expeditious loading of these cars is necessary as they temporarily block the Little Lakes Lines active branch line track during this process.

Front and right side elevations of the Poppa-Cow Dairy building are shown in Figure 1. Parts used in construction of this project are listed in Tables 1 through 4. A 4" x 11" x 1/2" piece of plywood provides a good base for the structure. The platform and structure are raised about 1 1/4 above the track bed to allow use with standard operating milk cars. A piece of sheet steel may be embedded in the trackside section of the platform to provide a grip surface for magnetic milk cans. Commercial model train milk car platforms have removable steel platforms. These could be cut for use as the steel base on the Poppa-Cow platform. Alternatively, the Poppa-Cow platform could be extended to accept an unmodified commercial unit.

Roadwork should be performed so that the access road is about level with an edge of the platform so that the "Bar F" Ranch trucks can make their deliveries and pick-ups. The building is constructed of 3/32" thick sheet balsa wood with all corners reinforced with 3/16" square stock. It has a wide opening facing the platform and a single window on the right side so that the man may be viewed when working inside. Either carve cinder block outlines into the building foundation or sim-

Table 1 Poppa-Cow Dairy Building Parts List

Quan.	Item	Description
1 ea	Plywood Base	4" x 11" x 1/2"
1 ea.	Balsa Wood	3/32" x 3" x 36"
1 ea.	Balsa Wood	3/16" x 3/16"x 36"
1 ea.	Balsa Wood	1/16" x 1/8"x 36"
1 ea.	Balsa Wood	1/16" x 1/16" x 36"
1 ea.	Window Frame	Plastic: (8 Pane, 3/4" x 1 1/2")
1 piece	Thin Plastic	≈ 1" x 2" Clear
1 sheet	Building Paper	Brick or Stone
1 ea.	Brass Tube	1/4" x 4 1/2" long (Smokestack)
1 piece	Steel Sheet	≈ 2" x 3"
1 ea.	Figure	Man holding milk can
8 ea.	Milk Cans	O Scale size
1 ea.	Balsa wood glue	Normal Drying
1 ea.	Paper glue	Clear-drying
Misc.	Acrylic paints	

ply cover it with brick or stone paper. Multiple advertising signs may be mounted on the exterior walls.

Figure 2 illustrates the "Man-with-Can" mechanism. It is assembled entirely from standard size brass strip stock. Very little cutting is required. Solder joints at the three locations shown in Figure 2 hold the drive assembly in position. As wheel #BT rotates, the entire assembly (with both man and guide arm) moves about 2" laterally. This distance is equal to two times the distance between the center of the drive disk, #BT, and the drive pin. Alignment is maintained by a combination of two

Table 2 Poppa-Cow Dairy Mechanical Parts List

Quan.	Item	Description
2 ea.	Pierced Disk	Erector #BT
1 ea.	Metal Strip	Erector #G (≈1¾" long)
2 ea.	Brass Strip	¼" x 1/16" x 12" (Support & Drive/Guide Arms)
1 ea.	Brass Strip	¼" x 1/32" x 12" (Bearing Strip)
1 ea.	Brass Tube	3/16" I.D. x 5/16" long (Drive Pin Bushing)
2 ea.	Brass Tube	3/16" I.D. x ¼" long (Drive Arm Guide Bushings)
2 ea.	Wood Screw	No. 8, ½" long (Drive Arm Guides)
4 ea.	Machine Screw	8-32, ½" long
1 ea.	Machine Screw	8-32, 1¼" long (Drive Pin)
7 ea.	Nut	8-32
5 ea.	Lockwasher	No. 8
2 ea.	Washer	No. 8 (Drive Pin Assembly)

Table 3 Poppa-Cow Dairy Electrical Parts List

Quan.	Item	Description
1 ea.	Circuit #1	12 VDC Component Set
1 ea.	Circuit #5	Component Set
1 ea.	Resistor	1 MΩ, ¼ watt
1 ea.	Resistor	2.2 MΩ, ¼ watt
1 ea.	Capacitor	10 µf, 16 VDC (Tantalum)
6 ea.	Lamp	12 Volt Grain-of-Wheat
2 ea.	Motor	2 rpm with ≈1/8" dia. shaft
2 ea.	Power Switch	SPST

Table 4   Circuit References & Electrical Values

Device	Reference	R_A	R_B	C
Relay Timer	Circuit #5	1.0 MΩ (¼ watt)	2.2 MΩ (¼ watt)	10 µf (16 VDC)

things. First, as seen in the Figure 2 Drive Pin Assembly Detail, washers on either side on the drive pin hold the 1/4" wide drive arm loop, in place. Allow for about 1/16" play. A brass bushing slipped over the 8-32 machine screw provides a smooth surface so that the screw threads cannot bind the mechanism. Second, There is a pair of brass bushing-covered No. 8 wood screws in the base to hold the lower guide arm true. A brass strip is also placed beneath the Drive Arm Assembly to ensure the whole unit will move smoothly as it travels back and forth. This is the only real weight-bearing surface as the support arm, with the man, "floats" slightly above the floor of the platform. Motor #1 moves the man. It is mounted so that the drive shaft is horizontal as may be seen in Figure 3. A wall may be built behind the man to

hide the mechanism. Just provide a small slot at the base of the wall to allow the flat support arm to move in and out.

Rotary conveyor construction is quite simple. A round wood base is glued onto disk #BT that is attached directly to vertically mounted motor #2 as shown in Figure 3. Fashion a cardstock cylinder and glue it to the round wood base. The cylinder and base may be painted black. This will make the silver milk cans glued to the base's perimeter much more obvious.

Poppa-Cow Dairy operation is controlled by the circuits shown in Figure 4. Motor #1, which moves the man carrying the can, occasionally stops to give the guy a rest! Sometimes he relaxes inside the building while at other times he pauses to catch a breath of fresh air. He really has a mind of his own! The milk can conveyor, driven by Motor #2, never pauses.

Lights are provided for loading cars far into the evening and early morning hours. The building's inte-

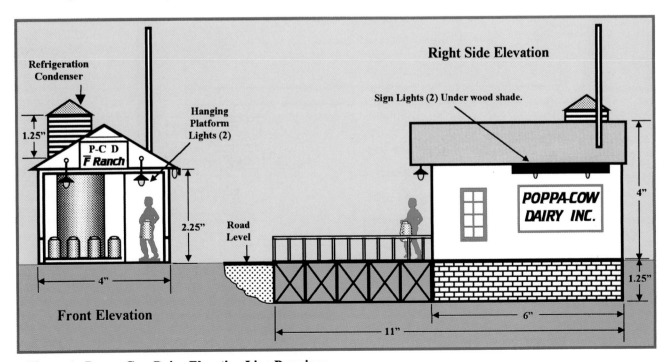

Figure 1 Poppa-Cow Dairy Elevation Line Drawings

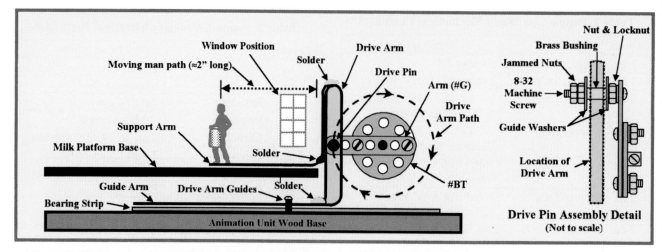

Figure 2   Poppa-Cow Dairy "Man-with-Can" Mechanism (Motor omitted for clarity.)

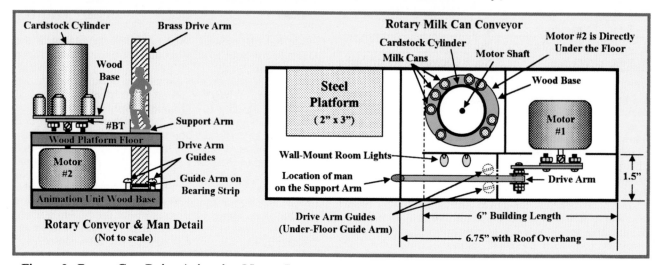

Figure 3   Poppa-Cow Dairy Animation Motors Layout

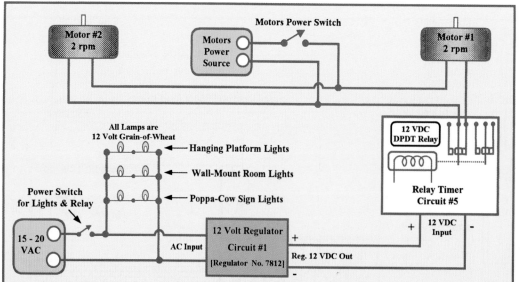

Figure 4   Poppa-Cow Dairy Wiring Diagram

by using wire lead grain-of-wheat lamps. Prior to hook-up, the wires may be fed through a small washer (e.g. #4) that serves as a light shade. Wiring the grain-of-wheat lamps in series, as shown, makes them run cooler and extends their life. It also results in a more realistic level of lighting for these directly viewed lights.

Installation of the Poppa-Cow Dairy on your layout adds considerable special interest to the already fascinating action of commercially produced operating milk cars. You would think that the Poppa-Cow dairyman would make every effort possible to get inside his building whenever that guy in the refrigerator car arrives and starts throwing those cans around!

rior is illuminated where the man runs about, the platform has two hanging lights, and the big Poppa-Cow sign on the right side of the building has two partially concealed "floodlights". Hanging lights are best made

Albert Music Hall
(This Project uses Electrical Circuit No. 6)

Waretown, NJ is home to the real Albert Music Hall. It is operated by the Pinelands Cultural Society; a non-profit, all volunteer organization dedicated to the preservation of the culture and musical traditions of the New Jersey Pinelands. Every Saturday night, all year long, live acoustic music concerts are presented. A place where all sorts of train songs such as: "Ridin' the New River Train", "Wabash Cannonball", "City of New Orleans", "Wreck of Old 97", and the old bluegrass favorite, "Orange Blossom Special" are still routinely performed!

Little Lakes Lines (LLL) inhabitants were never ones to miss a chance to enjoy themselves. Myriad local attractions such as the extensive Buena Vista Amusement Park, Podunk City's continuous John Philip Sousa band concerts in the square, and the Podunk Arts Theatre's Gilbert & Sullivan opera "H.M.S. Pinafore" already exist in the LLL's area. Consequently, considerable interest flourished when the opportunity arose to obtain their very own Albert Music Hall far out in the country. I am sure that the people on your layout too would enjoy their own version of this music hall.

Figure 1 shows the elevation line drawing and major dimensions of the model. The model is constructed of a balsa wood structure and roof with 1/8" clapboard wood sheet siding walls. Nine large windows consisting of plastic window frame inserts with clear plastic sheet "glass" provide for easy viewing of the interior. A basic parts list is provided in Table 1.

The building's exterior is painted New England red with white trim; the traditional Albert Music Hall colors.

Light blue is used on the interior walls. The roof is designed to represent metal, dark gray in color and showing signs of rust to suggest that this low cost structure has been in place for quite some time. It is constructed of 3/32" thick sheet balsa with 3/16" square ribs set at 1" intervals to represent metal roof standing seam joints. The smokestack located on the left rear part of the roof is a length of 3/16" O.D. brass tubing painted black. Pieces of 3/16" cove molding are used to finish the area where the roof meets the end gables.

Interior details deemed necessary to capture the aesthetics of the real Hall include the raised platform with large overhead speakers as shown in the Figure 1 stage interior view. The platform/stage is designed to resemble the interior of a rustic pinelands cabin. There is a 4' x 8' picture centered on the rear wall that represents a scene looking out the cabin window. Microphone stands for both instruments and vocalists are made of 1/32" diameter brass rod stock. Each stand consists of two sections of rod. On is for the vertical stand, the other for the adjustable "boom". The two pieces are cut to length, then crossed and soldered together at their intersection point. A blob of solder is placed at the end of each "boom" section to represent a microphone. The whole assembly may be painted silver to represent chrome. Four "monitor" speakers are placed along the front of the stage directed towards the performers. These are required in a live music show of this type as it allows the players to hear themselves and each other. The speakers are shaped pieces of balsa wood painted black. Other features include the sound mixing console, an old

Above: Three views of Albert Music Hall showing a) the front entrance; b) a view looking down into the theater; c) the stage and the performing artists.

upright piano and two log poles that were actually used to reinforce the roof of the original building. These are located as shown in the Figure 2 floor plan. Visible doors to the rear music practice/warm-up rooms and an admission ticket sales table on the porch are included.

A balsa wood frame consisting of both building end gables and the raised audience ceiling area holds all building lights and a 3" diameter audio speaker. The frame interlocks between the perimeter walls and the roof. It is not glued to either the walls or the roof to allow easy disassembly for access to the wiring connections.

Building lighting consists of 3 separate groups of lights. There are eight small 5 volt exterior front sign lights that provide for an even low-level illumination of the sign. As these lamps run cool, a dab of black latex paint may be placed directly on the bulb side opposite the sign to prevent glare to the on-looker's eyes. Inside, the six house lights are on a separate circuit from the seven stage lights. This will allow for extinguishing the house lights when the stage show commences.

The numerous signs used on the Albert Music Hall building were generated via computer and laser printer. The computer offers a simple and easy way to generate signs of most any font and point size. The font used for the large front Albert Music Hall sign is "Stagecoach". Of particular importance is the little sign on the right door, which lists the groups, performing at the current show. Signs may alternatively be made by hand, decals or dry transfer lettering. Calendars, showing the month of model building completion, are a signature of all Little Lakes Lines structures. The calendar dates are printed via computer. A suitable picture is then attached to the paper above the printing. Both the picture and the printed dates are then cut out as a unit and glued on to one of the interior walls.

Filling the Hall with many miniature people completes the scene. On the Little Lakes Lines, the volunteers are represented by ticket lady, Caroline, an Arttista figure with her rolls of colored tickets by the entrance door; the ever-popular 50-50 man, Marty, a Bachman figure outfitted in his characteristic straw hat with the hole in the top; and the sound engineer, Russ, a Circus Craft figure. Performers on the stage are "The Pineconers", represented via Arttista, Circus Craft, and Bowser figures outfitted with guitars and banjos. Suitable miniature guitars and banjos can be found in the form of pins, earrings and/or charms at shops that sell country & western style jewelry. The building has an audience of 43 persons seated on 1/4" scale folding chairs manufactured by Circus Craft.

Now is the time to fabricate the control system to bring the Albert Music Hall model to "life". A combination of light and sound is used to reproduce the ambiance of the prototype. While the house lights are

70

ON, the babble of the audience can be heard over the strains of songs recorded from earlier shows. Later upon your command, the house lights dim, the crowd hushes, and the music of the advertised performers is heard.

Figure 3 is an overview wiring diagram that illustrates the electrical control system. Two toggle switches are shown. One applies 5 volts for the lights; the other provides 12 VDC power to the audiocassette tape player. When both switches are closed, the house lights are ON and the audience/background music effect is heard. When the "Performance Pushbutton" is activated, the 12 volt DPDT Relay is energized. This switches the house lights and corresponding sounds OFF and simultaneously turns the current performer's music ON. The

Table 1 Albert Music Hall Building Parts List

Quan.	Item	Description
1 ea.	Balsa Wood	1/16" x 1/32"x 36"
1 ea.	Balsa Wood	1/4" x 1/4"x 36"
1 ea.	Balsa Wood	3/16" x 3/16" x 36"
1 ea.	Balsa Wood	3/32" x 3" x 36"
2 ea.	Wood Sheet	1/8" Clapboard 3" x 24"
11 ea.	Window Frames	Plastic: (8 Pane, ¾" x 1½")
2 ea.	Plastic Doors	
1 ea.	Balsa wood glue	Normal Drying
1 ea.	Paper glue	Clear-drying
1 ea.	Cove Molding	3/16" x 12"
1 sheet	Thin Plastic	8½" x 11" Clear
1 ea.	Brass Rod	12" x 1/32" Diameter
1 ea.	Brass Tube	12" x 3/16" Outside Dia.
Many	People	Seated & Standing
Many	Earrings/charms	Guitars & Banjos
Misc.	Acrylic paints	

Table 2 Albert Music Hall Electrical Parts List

Quan.	Item	Description
1 ea.	Speaker	3" Wide Range, 2 watts
1 ea.	Toggle Switch	SPST, 3 amps
1 ea.	Connector	6 Pin polarized male
1 ea.	Connector	6 Pin polarized female
1 ea.	Circuit #6	Component Set
1 ea.	Resistor	R=2.2 MΩ (¼ watt)
1 ea.	Capacitor	C_1=47 µf (16 vdc)
1 ea.	Capacitor	C_2=22 µf (16 vdc)
8 ea.	Lamps	#683, 5 volts, 60 ma.
13 ea.	Lamps	#330, 14 volts, 80 ma.
1 ea.	Cassette Tape Player	12 VDC with Auto-Reverse

Table 3 Circuit References & Electrical Values

Device	Reference	R	C
Relay Timer	Circuit #6	2.2 MΩ (¼ watt)	69 µf - Network (See Fig. 4)

Table 4 Equipment List for Creating the Albert Music Hall Master Tape

Quan.	Item	Identification No.	Typical Source(s)
1 each	Standard stereo system to play the source material and has tape recording capability. (Compact disk, phono, tape)		Probably existing around your house.
1 each	Additional Cassette Tape Player		Most discount, department, or electronics stores. Recording and auto-reverse features not required.
2 each	6' Shielded audio cable with phono connectors. (Plug to plug type.)	RS: 42-2367	Radio Shack (RS)
1 each	Shielded Y adapter. (Phono plug to 2 phono jacks type.)	RS: 42-2436	
4 each	Audio Recording Cassettes LN-90, Low Noise Ferric Type I (For individual and intermediate track combination recordings.)	RS: 44-912	
1 each	Audio Recording Cassettes LN-60, Low Noise Ferric Type I (For use as the Master Tape.)	RS: 44-911	
1 each	Recording of "crowd babble": Compact Disk by Major Records: "Sound Effects - Backgrounds"	(No number) ©1989 Thomas J. Valentino, Inc. RFT Music Publishing Corp., NY, NY	* See note below.
1 each	Intermission" Music	Your choice of music.	
1 each	"Performance" Music	Your choice of music.	

* Note: "Sound Effect" recordings typically contain a selection of 50 or more sounds. Consequently, each effect is usually a minute or less in duration.   It will therefore take many repeated recordings from the source to produce a complete 45 minute side of tape "A". This process is somewhat easier to perform using compact disk versions.

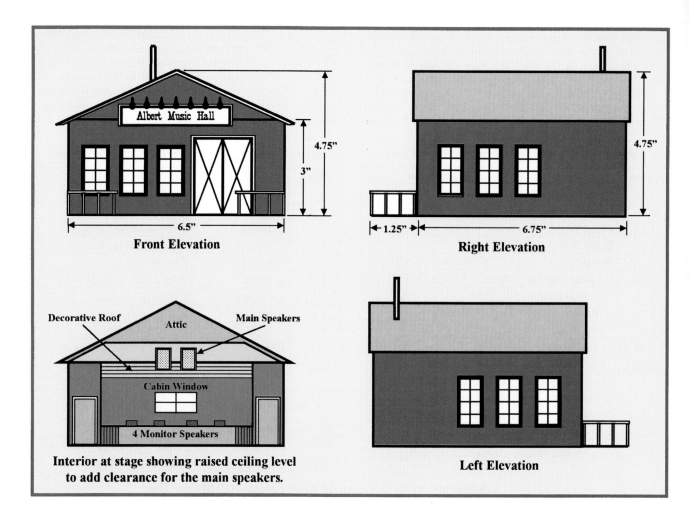

Front Elevation

4.75"

3"

6.5"

Right Elevation

4.75"

1.25"   6.75"

Decorative Roof   Attic   Main Speakers

Cabin Window

4 Monitor Speakers

Interior at stage showing raised ceiling level
to add clearance for the main speakers.

Left Elevation

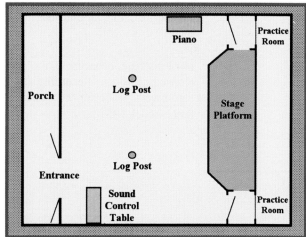

Practice Room

Piano

Porch

Log Post

Stage Platform

Entrance

Log Post

Sound Control Table

Practice Room

Figure 2 - Albert Music Hall Model Floor Plan

timer circuit maintains power to the relay for about 3 minutes. After this time period, the system resets to the "intermission" state until the "Performance Pushbutton" is momentarily pressed again. The major components of the control system are identified in Tables 2 and 3.

All wiring to the model building runs through a single six pin connector to allow for quick removal of the structure from the layout. Pins 1 and 2 are used for the speaker connections. Pin 3 is not used. Pins 4, 5, and 6 are used for the two light circuits with a common ground. The sign and stage lights are always ON when the main power is applied to the model. All lights are operated at

6 volts. Note that the 5 volt front sign lights are wired in "series" pairs, which makes them operate as if they were 10 volt lamps. I find that the illumination of the building and signs appears much more realistic when operating multiple lamps at about one half of their rated voltage.

"Pushbutton-Activated" Timer Circuit #6 is used to start the performance. The relay "hold-on" duration, of about 3 minutes, is determined by the 2.2 M resistor and the 69uf (47uf plus 22uf as shown in Figure 4) capacitor network. A separate 12 VDC source is needed for Circuit #6 and the audio tape player. Voltage regulation is optional.

An automobile cassette tape player is ideal to provide the sounds for this application. They operate from 12VDC and typically have the auto-reverse feature. This allows the tape to play continuously without attention. I recorded a half-hour of musical material before the songs are repeated. i.e. both sides of the hour cassette were made identical, only because it was easier. One could have an hour of listening without any material being repeated if so desired. An endless loop tape system could also be used except that such systems are normally limited to playing a mere 5 minutes before the recorded information repeats. It would be a mighty short show for a music hall model!

Creating the master tape for the player takes a bit of time and effort. Figure 5 illustrates the procedure. It is a matter of first re-recording each type of stereo material onto one-track (monaural) of an intermediate tape. Then, via use of two cassette tape players, simultane-

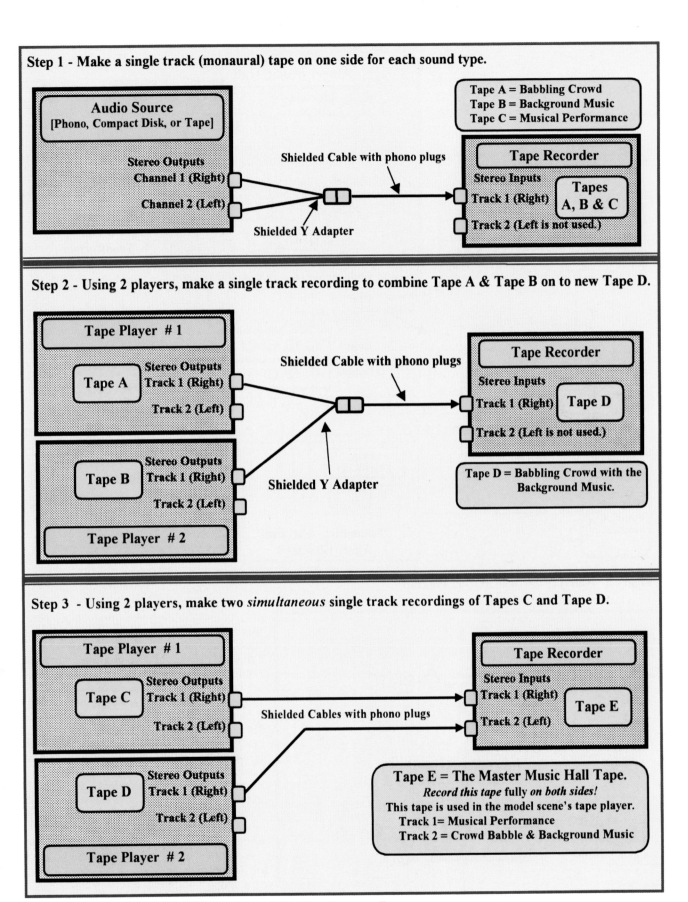

Figure 5 Albert Music Hall Master Tape "Creation Sequence"

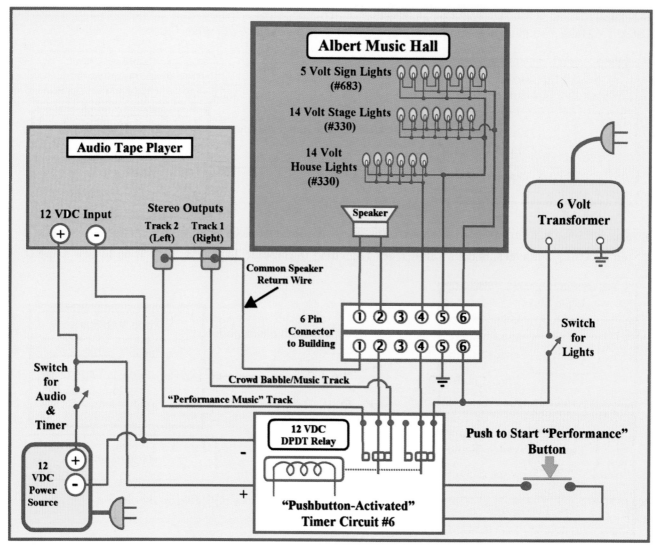

Figure 3   Albert Music Hall Wiring Diagram

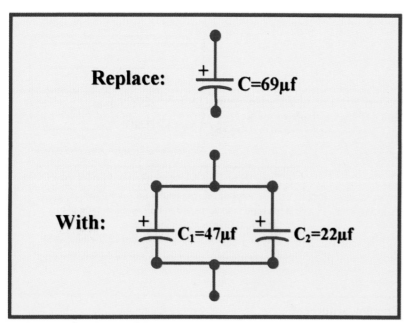

Figure 4   Timer #6 Capacitor Network

ously re-record the single-track intermediate tapes onto a two track (stereo) master "Music Hall" tape. I have identified the basic equipment that I used for my model in Table 4. Your hall could easily feature any type of music that you prefer. It could just as easily be a place for jazz musicians, rock bands or string quartets to play.

Once the circuitry is built and the master tape completed, the scene is ready for operation on your layout. Incidentally, my Albert Music Hall model may be seen briefly in OGR, the Video, Vol. 2, No. 2, Winter 1995 with the "performance" tape of the "Pineconers" playing for the audience. I hope that your miniature people enjoy their hall as much as those tiny individuals do on my Little Lakes Lines.

Chapter Seven

Railroad Yard Animations

Almost every layout has a railroad yard. It may consist of a lone station building or it may also include a siding or two for locomotive servicing and rolling stock storage. Others become increasingly elaborate and include extensive servicing facilities such as water towers, turntables with round houses, coal tipples, diesel fueling facilities, etc. However large or small a yard may be, animation is normally limited to the shuffling of locomotives and the passing of trains. This does not have to be the case. There are plenty of opportunities to add vitality to your railroad yard, even when there are no locomotives in sight! Four animated scenes that can do just that, are described in this chapter.

First, there is a hobo jungle huddled at the base of a floodlight tower in a remote section of the LLL's railroad yard. Here on a cool night you can see a group of these crusty high rail sentinels gathered close around a burning barrel for warmth. A pulsating red glow can be seen as profuse smoke rises skyward from the burning waste in the barrel.

Secondly, there is considerable early morning activity across the tracks at the Seaboard Ice Company. Huge blocks of ice are being moved by conveyor along the high illuminated icing platform. They are being set into position for loading into the roof hatches of a string of awaiting reefers.

Next, we find a group of exhausted gandy dancers in the far back of the railroad yard. They have just finished replacing a load of decayed crossties. The removed ties are now stacked in a pile to be burned. A flip of a switch and the old ties are ablaze! Burning embers and fingers of flame wrapped in thick clouds of smoke bring this scene to life time and time again. It is strange however, that with such a ferocious fire, this pile of ties never seems to get any smaller! No wonder the workers are becoming weary. They can't go home until the ties are ashes!

Lastly, there is the animated switch tower located at the railroad yard throat. Vigilant operators scanning train spotting and turnout setting indicators on the track diagram panel can be seen through the large windows. The constantly changing lights require a watchful eye to assure each train proceeds as planned. Interest is heightened if the track diagrams on these panels reflect the configuration of your own layout.

Read on and gather some more ideas to enliven your own yard area. If real estate is a problem, animated scenes like the hobo's barrel and the burning railroad ties take only a few square inches of layout space. The interest to inches ratio is well nigh unbeatable!

Hobo Jungle Burning Barrel
(This Project uses Electrical Circuits No. 1, No.6 and three No. 3 Circuits)

Nights tend to be chilly on model railroads. Consequently, a burning barrel is often seen as a source of warmth around typical hobo jungles. It usually consists of a fire made of waste, wood scraps and whatever all dumped into a standard 55 gallon oil drum. Such a scene may be easily reproduced in miniature and brought to "life" via use of light and smoke animation. The basic operational approach is to let the fire glow continuously. Smoke may be activated by visitors pressing a button to allow it to emerge for about one minute. Visitor control of the smoke is desirable as (1) visitors enjoy operating things, (2) smoke units do run dry and (3) there is little value in filling your train room with smoke when no one is paying attention to its source.

Figure 1 shows the basic configuration of the fire barrel. Major parts required to build the burning barrel are listed in Table 1. The barrel may be any one of the many hollow O-gauge plastic barrels or "oil drums" readily available at railroad hobby stores. It could also be fashioned from card stock or brass tubing. The bar-

rel should also have a lid that can be adjusted at an angle to allow the smoke to escape and to let the viewer see the glow of the fire without directly seeing the light bulbs. An assembly of three flickering miniature red lights mounted below the base of the visible barrel represents the "fire". Smoke is created by a Seuthe smoke generator located beneath the light assembly. Unfortunately, smoke does not readily flow from these generators when one extends the smoke path by placing a tube extension (such as a barrel) on them. A small fan and air pipe assembly is therefore needed to force air down into the Seuthe smoke generator that will, in turn, make the smoke flow up and out of the barrel.

Three light bulbs, used to simulate the flickering fire glow, are supported via a short section of 3/8" diameter brass metal tubing located between the smoke generator and the barrel as shown in Figure 2. The lamps are first tinted with transparent red glass paint. Holes

Table 1   Burning Barrel Parts List

Quan.	Item	Description
1 ea.	O Scale Barrel	Hollow, any material. (About 3/8" diameter)
1 ea.	Seuthe #6 Smoke Generator	14 Volt Max., 140 ma. (About 3/8" diameter)
12"	Brass tubing	1/8" Diameter
12"	Brass tubing	3/32" Diameter
1"	Brass tubing	3/8" Diameter
3 ea.	Lamp	#683, 5 Volts, 60 ma.
1 ea	Glass paint	Transparent red
1 ea.	Micro Fan	12 VDC, 150 ma.
1 ea.	Power Switch	SPST
1 ea.	Pushbutton	Normally Open
1 ea.	Circuit # 1	12 VDC Component Set
3 ea.	Circuit # 3	Component Set
1 ea.	Circuit # 6	Component Set
3 ea.	Diode	1N4001, 50 PIV, 1 Amp
4 ea.	Resistor	100 Ω, ½ watt
1 ea.	Resistor	6.8 KΩ, ¼ watt
2 ea.	Resistor	8.2 KΩ, ¼ watt
1 ea.	Resistor	33 KΩ, ¼ watt
1 ea.	Resistor	47 KΩ, ¼ watt
1 ea.	Resistor	82 KΩ, ¼ watt
1 ea.	Resistor	2.2 MΩ, ¼ watt
3 ea.	Capacitor	2.2 μf, 16 VDC (Tantalum)
1 ea.	Capacitor	22 μf, 16 VDC (Tantalum)

Table 2   Circuit References & Electrical Values

Device	Reference	R_A	R_B	C
Lamp #1 Timer	Circuit #3	82 KΩ (¼ watt)	8.2 KΩ (¼ watt)	2.2 μf (16 VDC)
Lamp #2 Timer	Circuit #3	33 KΩ (¼ watt)	6.8 KΩ (¼ watt)	2.2 μf (16 VDC)
Lamp #3 Timer	Circuit #3	47 KΩ (¼ watt)	8.2 KΩ (¼ watt)	2.2 μf (16 VDC)
Relay Timer	Circuit #6	R=2.2 MΩ (¼ watt)	N/A	22 μf (16 VDC)

are drilled in the metal tube for the three lamps. A 3/32" diameter metal tube for the airflow should be bent to shape as shown in Figure 1. It should extend about half way down inside the smoke generator, but not so far as to become submerged in the smoke fluid when the unit is loaded. A small notch must be cut into the brass lamp support ring to allow this tube to be properly positioned. Next, the painted lamps are glued in place and lead wires are attached. The brass tube ring with the lights is then fitted to the top of the smoke generator. It may be held in place by binding it to the upper part of the smoke generator with electrical tape. Alternatively, the ring could be secured in position by using epoxy or glue although this will make any future maintenance of the smoke unit or lamps more difficult.

A small air-tight box with a fan mounted on one end and a 1/8" diameter brass tube on the other serves as a low, but sufficient, air pressure supply to coax the generated smoke to emerge from the fire barrel section. The 3/32" diameter air flow tube slides inside the larger 1/8" tube. An overlap of an inch or so forms an adequate seal for this application while facilitating easy separation of the two assemblies. A hole to clear the 3/8" brass ring must then be drilled in the train layout tabletop. The unit may be fastened in several ways via angle clamps, epoxy, etc. The barrel itself rests on top with a little dab of glue to hold it in place. Leave the barrel's lid removable to allow convenient access for filling it with smoke fluid.

Figure 3 illustrates the wiring of the burning barrel. A 12 VDC Regulator is used so that any voltage between 15 to 20 VAC may be used to power this item. The regulator assures that a good volume of smoke will be produced while simultaneously protecting the smoke generator and lamps from being over-stressed. A single switch controls the fire glow while the smoke feature is activated by via the pushbutton. Each of the "fire" lamps independently flickers at different rates to give a convincing "burning" glow effect. This is done by use of

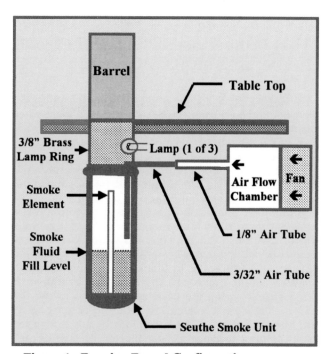

Figure 1   Burning Barrel Configuration

three separate lamp timer circuits. Note that these timers allow the lamp to be more "ON" than "OFF", a feature that enhances the burning effects. The pushbutton-initiated smoke effect is maintained for about one minute by a timed relay that controls both the smoke generator and the fan. Specific component values for each of the timer circuits are defined in Table 2.

Upon testing the unit and installation, your hobo jungle setting is ready for the finishing touches. The ground area would very likely consist of cinders and ashes with a few struggling weeds appearing here and there. Hobo figures are available from Arttista and numerous other sources. To increase interest in your scene, add some hobos playing guitars. Others could be happily listening and drinking their bottles of diet sassafras tea. Placing a couple of operating lanterns around will heighten the nighttime effect. (See Bibliography for information sources for operating lantern fabrication.) A final thought is that a small audio speaker could be concealed nearby, perhaps under a pile of cinders. Here, "Woody Guthrie type" railroad songs could be played via a standard auto-reverse tape player. Your "jungle" will really spring to life as your guitar strumming and singing hobos, lounge by their warm & smoky burning barrel, with softly glowing lanterns. It is almost enough to make you want to "ride-the-rods" yourself and join their world.

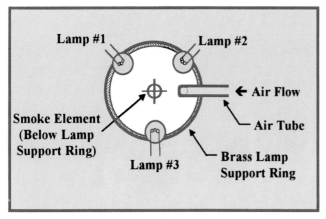

Figure 2 Lamp Support Ring Detail (Top View)

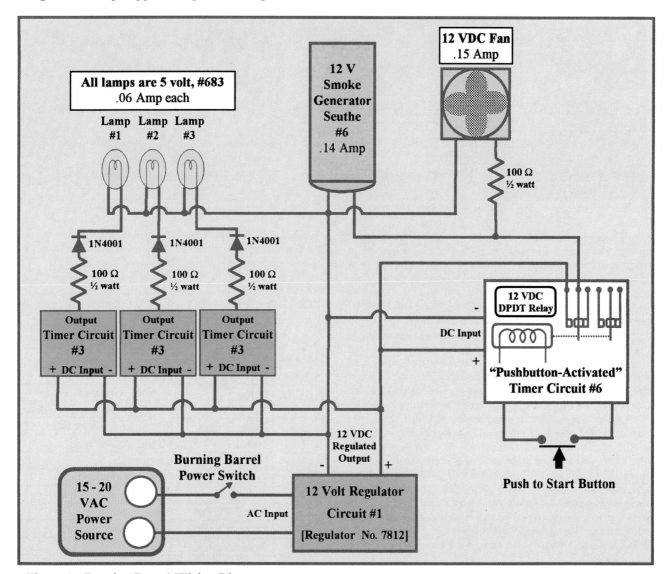

Figure 3 Burning Barrel Wiring Diagram

Seaboard Ice Company

Back in the days before the advent of mechanical refrigerator cars, railroads shipped perishable goods in insulated cars cooled by blocks of ice. The ice was loaded into the cars via roof hatches located at each end. Icehouses were spotted at various points along the railroad route to provide the capability of keeping the cars cool and their perishable cargo from spoiling.

The earliest facilities consisted of icehouses where blocks of ice sawed were from ponds in the winter and stored for later use. Second generation icehouses had bulky mechanical refrigeration equipment that enabled them to make block ice on site. The Seaboard Ice Company on the Little Lakes Lines is such a building. Notice the large cooling condensers on the roof of the structure. There is a long raised deck that runs parallel to the tracks where cars requiring ice can be spotted. The Seaboard Ice Company model is configured to automatically distribute the large blocks of ice along the deck at refrigerator car roof level. When the ice moves to the proper position, a worker on the platform uses a long iron bar to push it over and into the waiting car's open roof hatch. The model shown here has a 23" long (92 scale feet) top deck which can simultaneously service two cars.

The Seaboard Ice Company business offices and ice-making equipment reside in the building section that houses the motor drive mechanism that drags the ice blocks along the platform. The size and shape of the motor somewhat dictates the size of the building.

A 3 3/4" wide by 27 1/2" long solid wood base made from a 1" thick pine board forms the base for this model. This provides a sturdy base on which to construct the

Table 1 Seaboard Ice Company Parts List

Quan.	Item	Description
20 ea.	Ice Block	Lucite blocks
12 ea.	Lamp	16 Volt, Grain-of-Wheat
2 ea.	Lamp	#1445, 18 Volt, bayonet base
2 ea.	Lamp Socket	Miniature Bayonet Base
1 ea.	Motor	Miniature, ≈ 2 rpm
1 ea.	Flanged Wheel	Erector #Z
1 ea.	Sheave Pulley	Erector #AQ
1 ea.	Axle Rod	Erector #P57A, 2 1/8" long
6'	Heavy Thread	Black, Upholstery
1 ea.	Tension Spring	≈ 3/32" diameter, 1/2" long
2 ea.	Power Switch	SPST
1 ea.	Connector	3 pin polarized male
1 ea.	Connector	3 pin polarized female

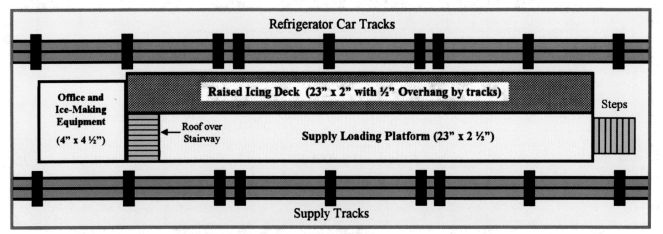

Figure 1   Seaboard Ice Company Physical Layout (Top View)

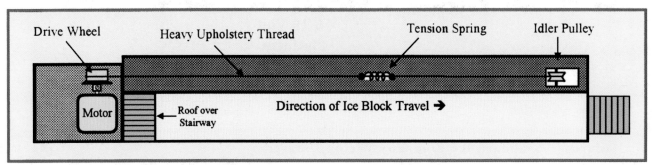

Figure 2   Ice Moving Mechanism (Top View)

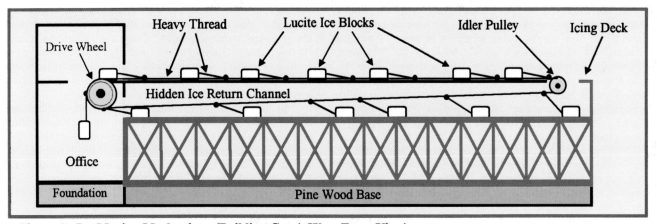

Figure 3   Ice Moving Mechanism (Building Cut-A-Way, Front View)

rather delicate raised icing platform deck. The entire model is designed as a removable unit that electrically plugs into the layout. Being easily removable simplifies construction and any future maintenance that may be required.

The box car door height loading platform is made from a 4" wide sheet of 3/32" thick balsa. The office is also constructed of 3/32" thick sheet balsa with commercial windows and homemade balsa doors. Pieces of 1/4" thick sheet balsa, scribed to represent a cement block foundation are glued to the pine base beneath the building area. Various sizes of balsa strips are used for applications including corner bracing (3/16" square), roofing planks (3/16" x 1/16"), icing platform supports (1/8"

square), and icing platform cross bracing (1/16" square). Everything is held together with slow drying balsa wood glue.

Major components used to animate the Seaboard Ice Company are listed in Table 1. Figure 1 illustrates the physical layout of the structure. Figures 2 and 3 show the ice moving mechanism. A low voltage slow-moving motor is fitted with an Erector #Z flanged wheel or equivalent. This wheel will be driving a heavy thread belt which runs the length of the deck to an idler pulley, Erector #AQ, and back. A light belt tension should be maintained by use of a short, small diameter, tension spring. The drive wheel has a fairly wide flat surface area which inherently provides a smooth way for the dan-

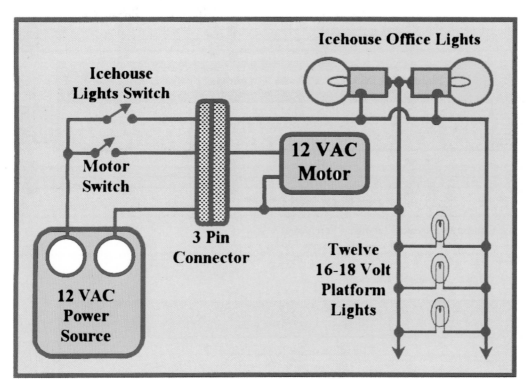

Figure 4   Seaboard Ice Company Wiring Diagram

gling ice blocks to be positioned back onto the upper deck as may be seen in Figure 3. It is wise to cover the metal flat area of the drive wheel with some sort of a rough-backed tape, such as electrician's friction tape. This will serve to reduce slipping of the thread belt. The idler pulley is mounted on a short metal shaft, e.g. Erector axle rod. Both ends of the shaft are embedded in the balsa wood structure. Small spacing washers may be used on either side of the idler pulley to assure that it remains free moving.

Ice blocks are formed from small clear Lucite pieces with all edges filed smooth. The smooth rounded edges are necessary to eliminate any snagging of the blocks on their travels through the model. They also more realistically portray the look of slightly melting ice.   The ice blocks are tethered to the main belt by approximately one half-inch long pieces of thread.   One end of the thread is glued directly to the ice block. The other end is both tied and glued to the upholstery thread "belt".

As may be seen in Figure 3, the driven belt drags the ice blocks across the top deck in a direction away from the icehouse where they are manufactured. When the

blocks reach the idler pulley, they fall into the beginning of the ice block return channel that is concealed within the platform superstructure. There they ride on the top of the hidden channel until they finally swing free in a hidden section behind the office area. Finally, they are hoisted up over the wide drive wheel where they again emerge from the icehouse on the top deck.

Eleven 16 volt grain-of-wheat lamps with metal shields are evenly spaced along the icing deck and about the loading platform areas for nighttime operation. An additional light hangs over the office door. Two 18 volt miniature bayonet base lamps are mounted in sockets to illuminate the interior of the office.

Wiring, as shown in Figure 4, is straightforward. The motor and lights on the Little Lakes Lines model all operate from 12 volts AC. Consequently, a three pin connector is sufficient to make the model removable from the layout. The lights and motor are controlled via separate switches.

One might say that an operating icehouse, such as this, has got to be the "coolest" animation on the entire layout!

Burning Railroad Ties
(This Project uses Electrical Circuits No. 1, No. 2 and three No. 4 Circuits)

Every year, real railroads must replace thousands of deteriorating track ties. Piles of ties quickly materialize when the work crew is finished refurbishing a track section. The roadbed is often strewn with many piles of old ties. The Little Lakes Lines is no exception. But what can one do with all those old ties? The LLL's environmentally incorrect method of disposal is to burn the ties, a practice once done by the real railroads. The creosote burns well. It makes a nice hot smoky fire for the workmen to gather 'round, warm themselves, drink their coffee, and tell their stories.

A pile of burning ties makes an interesting model. Your pile of ties will spew smoke and produce a very realistic flame and smoldering ember effect. This model is even more impressive at night when the traces of flickering flames project upon the rising clouds of smoke to make it appear that the ties are being consumed.

Modeling the pile of ties is easy. Just stack and glue ten pieces of wood painted and dimensioned as the other track cross ties on your layout into a pile. They are arranged in four levels as may be seen in the photo. The lower two layers have three ties each while the upper two consist of just two ties each. Careful attention should be given to their alignment to assure that the fire lamps are concealed from direct view. Open spaces between ties should allow for only the smoke and indirect illumination from the fire lamps to escape.

Table 1 lists the parts required for this model. Figure 1 illustrates its basic configuration. A 1-1/2" diameter hole should be cut in the table for this animation. The entire light, fan, and smoke unit assembly may be mounted in an open-top project box, either plastic or metal, beneath the hole as shown in Figure 1. When complete, it can be fastened to the underside of the table via small angle brackets.

Table 1 Burning Railroad Ties Parts List

Quan.	Item	Description
10 ea.	Wood Tie	Wood, painted black.
8 ea.	Lamp	#330, 14 Volts, 80 ma.
1 ea.	Glass paint	Transparent Red & Amber
1 ea.	Wire-wound Smoke Unit	Heater resistor with fiberglass wick cover.
1 ea.	Kerosene Lamp Wick	Fiberglass ≈ 6" length x 1" wide
1 ea.	Glass Jar	≈ 10 FL Oz. w/Screw Lid
1 ea.	Project Box	≈ 6" x 3" x 2"
4 ea.	Angle Bracket	1" ("L" Corner Brace)
1 ea.	Micro Fan	12 VDC, 150 ma.
12"	Tubing	5/16" Heat Shrink
2 ea.	Power Switch	SPST
1 ea.	Circuit # 1	12 VDC Component Set
3 ea.	Circuit # 4	Component Set
1 ea.	Circuit # 2	Component Set
1 ea	Resistor	150 Ω, 10 watt
1 ea	Resistor	5.6 KΩ, 1/4 watt
1 ea	Resistor	6.8 KΩ, 1/4 watt
1 ea	Resistor	10 KΩ, 1/4 watt
1 ea	Resistor	33 KΩ, 1/4 watt
1 ea	Resistor	47 KΩ, 1/4 watt
1 ea	Resistor	68 KΩ, 1/4 watt
1 ea	Resistor	100 KΩ, 1/4 watt
1 ea	Resistor	680 KΩ, 1/4 watt
3 ea.	Capacitor	2.2 µf, 16 VDC (Tantalum)
1 ea.	Capacitor	10 µf, 16 VDC (Tantalum)

Table 2   Circuit References & Electrical Values

Device	Reference	R_A	R_B	C
Lamps #1 & #2 Timer	Circuit #4	5.6 KΩ (¼ watt)	33 KΩ (¼ watt)	2.2 µf (16 VDC)
Lamps #3 & #4 Timer	Circuit #4	6.8 KΩ (¼ watt)	47 KΩ (¼ watt)	2.2 µf (16 VDC)
Lamps #5 & #6 Timer	Circuit #4	10 KΩ (¼ watt)	68 KΩ (¼ watt)	2.2 µf (16 VDC)
Fan Timer	Circuit #2	100 KΩ (¼ watt)	680 KΩ (¼ watt)	10 µf (16 VDC)

Now make the necessary openings in the project box. Drill holes to secure the four angle brackets around the open top rim of the box. Position the brackets so that it may be securely mounted against the bottom of the table. This must be a reasonably tight fit to ensure that the smoke will not escape from around the edges. Next drill holes to mount the micro-fan. Additional openings must be made, as required, to allow the fans airflow to enter the project box chamber. Holes to secure the lid of a small jar should be made in the bottom of the box. A larger hole in the lid's center is needed for passage of the smoke fluid wick. Two additional holes are needed in the side of the project box for the electrical wires. Once the wires are in place, any remaining gaps should be sealed via tape or epoxy to prevent smoke loss.

The eight fire lamps can be made as a cluster supported by their own wires. They must be electrically insulated from each other via small pieces of 5/16" heat shrink tubing. When in position, there should be plenty of air gap space around the lamps so that the smoke from the unit below can flow up and out.

The eight lamp assembly is wired in accordance with Figure 2. Table 2 specifies the component values for each timer circuit. Two red lamps will constantly glow dim to play the part of "embers". The other six will each flicker at a different rate and be considerably brighter to represent flames. Color three of these lamps red and the remaining lamps amber. A total of eleven different wires will emerge from this bundle for connection to the electronics. It is best to use solid wires, (#22 gauge is good), with multi-colored insulation. Solid wires provide superior support for the assembly above the smoke unit

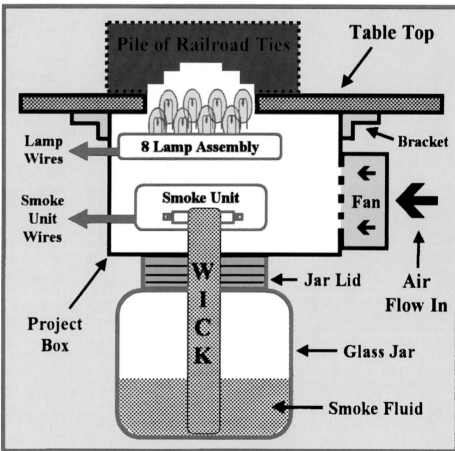

Figure 1   Burning Railroad Ties Configuration

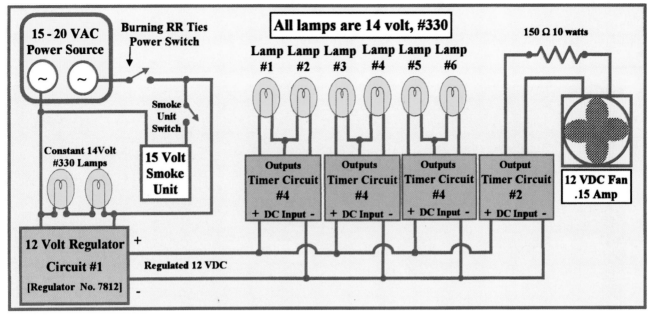

Figure 2   Burning Railroad Ties Wiring Diagram

and the colors will help you track individual wires when bundled. Wires may be easily soldered directly to the midget flange base lamps to avoid the need for space-consuming sockets. When in final position, the eight lamp assembly should be located within the 1 1/2" diameter hole with some of the lamps rising slightly above the top of the table.

The smoke unit is a standard wire wound smoke unit resistor element commonly used in older toy trains. They often come with a fiberglass wick sleeve. Leave this covering on, loop the long fiberglass wick around it and feed the wick through the project box bottom and glass jar lid. The wick material is normally sufficiently stiff to make the smoke element self-supporting. If not, additional pieces of solid wire may be used as reinforcement. Make sure that the wick reaches well down to the bottom of the jar. There is no such thing as too much wick! Solder the connecting wires to the resistor, route them through the side of the project box and connect them as shown in wiring diagram.

With all parts mounted and tested, proceed to attach the completed project box assembly to the underside of the table via screws through the four angle brackets. Wet the fiberglass wick with smoke fluid. Put additional fluid in the jar and screw the jar onto the lid. Filling the jar about 1/3 full will probably give you years of intense smoking operation without further attention.

I recommend that two separate switches be used to control this model scene as shown in Figure 2. One for the flickering lights which you may wish to have run most of the time. The second for the smoke unit, that you may want to curtail before your train room becomes too foggy.

In operation, the smoke will slowly develop as the fire burns. The fire will flare up when the fan operates and die down during the off cycle. Fortunately, the smoke effect cycling also helps to slow down the "fogging" of your train room!

Switch Tower T-1
(This Project uses Electrical Circuit No. 1 and four or more No. 4 Circuits

Railroad yards operate under the vigilant eyes of the men in the switch tower. They are constantly aware of the train schedules and position of each train under their purview. T-1 is the busiest tower on the Little Lakes Lines. It is located at the entrance to the Podunk railroad yard. Long haul passenger and freight trains constantly arrive and depart. There is considerable local traffic too as locomotive servicing, industrial switching and icehouse operations all must occasionally share trackage in this most active area. The tower men must quickly and accurately set the turnouts to assure safe passage for all trains while keeping delays to a minimum.

Two large indicator/control panels are housed in Tower T-1 to assist the men in their work. They contain a diagram of immediate and surrounding area trackage as illustrated in Figure 1. Numerous red indicator lights are mounted on the panel's diagrams. The lights wink on and off as turnouts are set and trains pass through them. Characteristically large observation windows provide the miniature operators with an unobstructed view of the Podunk rail yard. They also provide full-size visitors with an excellent view of the tower's interior. Watching the many panel indicators glow red and then darken gives you an intrinsic understanding of the ceaseless activity that is surely taking place on your railroad!

Tower T-1 is a plain rectangular building made of 3/32" thick sheet balsa with 3/16" square balsa internal bracing. The side walls are covered with three-dimensional brick and stone vinyl sheet material. Two large

Table 1   Tower T-1 Parts List

Quan.	Item	Description
8 ea.	Lamp	#683, 5 Volts, 60 ma.
1 ea.	Glass paint	Transparent Red
1 ea.	Power Switch	SPST
1 ea.	Circuit # 1	5 VDC Component Set
4 ea.	Circuit # 4	Component Set
2 ea.	Resistor	470 KΩ, ¼ watt
4 ea.	Resistor	1.0 MΩ, ¼ watt
2 ea.	Resistor	2.2 MΩ, ¼ watt
4 ea.	Capacitor	10 µf, 16 VDC (Tantalum)
24"	Tubing	3/64" Heat Shrink
12"	Tubing	1/8" Heat Shrink

indicator panels, office furniture, desk lamps, a potbelly stove, and the tireless tower men are readily visible through the large clear plastic windows.

The focus here is upon construction of the operating routing indicator panel. One or more of these panels may be placed in a tower depending upon its specific dimensions. Commercially available switch and signal tower kits may be used in lieu of constructing your own building from scratch. The floor and panel assembly discussed in the following paragraphs can be easily made to fit into any number of standard tower designs.

Components necessary to make an operational indi-

Table 2   Circuit References & Electrical Values

Device	Reference	R_A	R_B	C
Lamps #1 & #2 Timer	Circuit #4	1.0 MΩ (¼ watt)	470 KΩ (¼ watt)	10 µf (16 VDC)
Lamps #3 & #4 Timer	Circuit #4	1.0 MΩ (¼ watt)	1.0 MΩ (¼ watt)	10 µf (16 VDC)
Lamps #5 & #6 Timer	Circuit #4	2.2 MΩ (¼ watt)	470 KΩ (¼ watt)	10 µf (16 VDC)
Lamps #7 & #8 Timer	Circuit #4	2.2 MΩ (¼ watt)	1.0 MΩ (¼ watt)	10 µf (16 VDC)

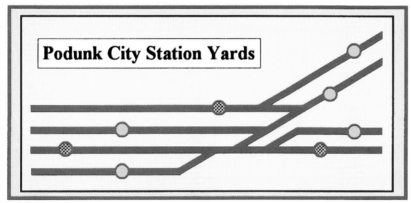

Figure 1   Typical Panel Diagram

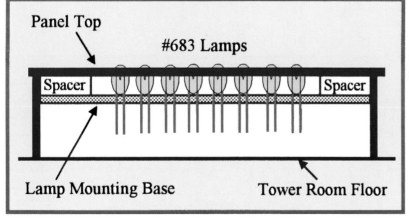

Figure 2   Typical Panel Configuration (Side View)

cator panel are listed in Table 1. The panel top is 3/32" sheet balsa cut to your desired dimensions. It is then painted off-white with acrylic paint. When dry, paint your track diagram in a contrasting color. Next, locate those points on the diagram where you wish to place indicator lamps. Drill holes through the panel at each indicator location using a bit slightly smaller than the size of the #683 light bulbs. Cut a second piece of 3/32" sheet balsa for use as a lamp-mounting base. Lay the top panel upon the lamp-mounting base. Make a small mark through each drilled hole onto the mounting base via a

sharp pencil. At each marked location, insert a #683 lamp by carefully pushing the bulb's wire leads through the balsa wood as shown in Figure 2. A straight pin may be used to first make a clearance hole for the wire leads to prevent their bending. Check that the wire leads of each lamp are well separated. This will facilitate later wire attachment and serve to avoid the chance of the wires electrically shorting together. These lamps run very cool so their close proximity to the wood is not a concern. A small dab of glue may be used at the base of each bulb to hold it in position. Mount all of the lamps to the base in this manner. This is an ideal time to paint them with the transparent red glass paint as they are held fast in an upright position.

Make some small spacers out of balsa wood scraps and glue them in place to create the configuration depicted in Figure 2. Just the very top of the mounted lamps should emerge from the drilled holes in the top panel when the two units are aligned. Finish the assembly by adding side pieces to create a desk-like look.

Solder approximately three foot lengths of flexible #22 or #24 size wires to extend the lamp leads. Work fairly quickly with a low wattage iron to avoid scorching the lamp-mounting base. Slip a half-inch long piece of heat shrink tubing over each soldered lamp lead joint as further insurance against electrical shorts. Fabricate each two-lamp assembly as shown in Figure 3. Note that two wires are common for each pair of lamps. Use a wire of a different color for this common connection. Once soldered and the heat shrink tubing is in place, gently twist the common and the remaining two wires for each lamp pair together. The tubing may be held in position against the lamp-mounting base via application of glue or epoxy. This will also serve as a strain relief when you get to the point of squishing the nest of wires into the final structure and on out to the electronic timer location. When done, there should be a number of three feet long, twisted, three wire groups, each with an identifiable common wire. Figure 4 shows the overall-wiring scheme where four three-wire groups are illustrated. One group connects to each timer

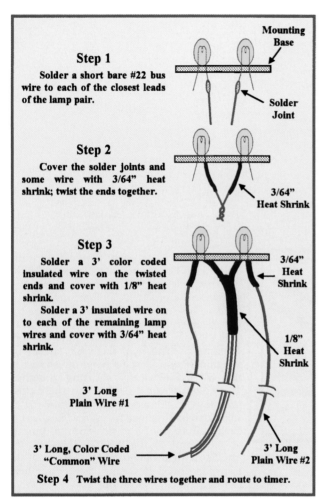

Step 1

Solder a short bare #22 bus wire to each of the closest leads of the lamp pair.

Mounting Base

Solder Joint

Step 2

Cover the solder joints and some wire with 3/64" heat shrink; twist the ends together.

3/64" Heat Shrink

Step 3

Solder a 3' color coded insulated wire on the twisted ends and cover with 1/8" heat shrink.

Solder a 3' insulated wire on to each of the remaining lamp wires and cover with 3/64" heat shrink.

3/64" Heat Shrink

1/8" Heat Shrink

3' Long Plain Wire #1

3' Long, Color Coded "Common" Wire

3' Long Plain Wire #2

Step 4 Twist the three wires together and route to timer.

Figure 3 Two Lamp Group Assembly Detail

circuit. It does not matter which group goes to which timer. Depending on your degree of ambition, the regulator can drive six additional timer circuits to support a total panel population of 20 indicator lights! Connectors may be optionally installed on the wires to facilitate future tower removal from the layout. Table 2 provides the values for use in the four indicator control timer circuits.

Cut another piece of 3/32" sheet balsa to the dimensions of the entire tower floor area. Make an opening in the floor beneath the panel unit. Glue the panel unit to the floor. Feed the three-wire bundles through the floor opening. There should be plenty of room in the tower structure for the wires due to the panel's second floor location. All other details such as desks and people, even additional room area lighting, may be added to the floor area at this time.

Finally, complete the exterior of the tower structure. Then slip the completed interior floor with details, wiring, and indicator panels into place. It may be retained in position within the tower via glue or removable balsa wood framing. Complete the wiring to the switch and transformer per Figure 4. The circuit boards may be mounted within the tower if space permits, camouflaged in an adjacent building by scenery on top of the layout board, or mounted underneath the layout table.

Find some suitable real estate within view of your yard tracks and install the tower. Turn on the switch and watch your automatic indicator panels go into action. You can sit back and relax, as your watchful tower men should now have no problem in keeping your trains correctly routed and on schedule!

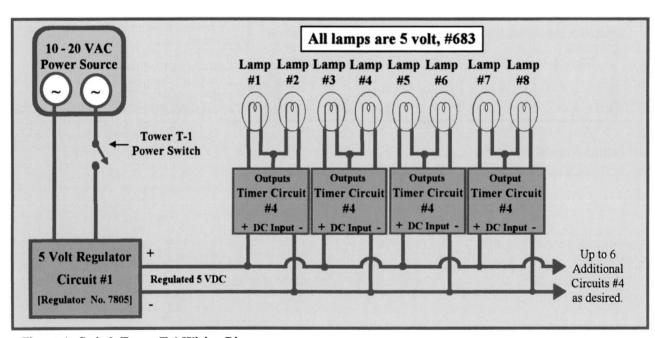

Figure 4 Switch Tower T-1 Wiring Diagram

Chapter Eight

Material Sources

Materials from countless individual sources are used to build and to complement the Little Lakes Lines animated scenes. Some of the sources that I have repeatedly used are identified in the following tables. Many things, however, due to their unusual or specialized nature may be "typically" found in certain "types" of stores. These have been so identified to that rudimentary extent in the text. Various items can be routinely found in your neighborhood hobby store and in model railroad publication advertisements.

Full addresses and telephone numbers of some specific material suppliers are listed in Table 1. Addresses, phone numbers, and Internet web addresses are provided. These companies offer catalogs and do business by mail order.

Electrical materials used in fabrication of animation control circuits are alphabetically listed in Table 2. Multiple sources are provided for the major electrical items. This information is current at time of printing. The vast majority of the listed items have been in exis-

tence for many years. Whereas "item numbers" are anticipated to remain relatively constant, specific vendor "stock" and "catalog part" numbers may be expected to change over time. There are many substitution possibilities with the electric parts. Capacitors with higher voltage ratings, resistors with higher wattage ratings and diodes with higher current and PIV ratings can be readily exchanged.

Although the use of standard Erector Set pieces is extremely convenient, it is possible to construct brass or other metal substitutes. Components such as setscrew collars for 1/8" shafts can be found in the airplane section of most hobby shops. Table 3 identifies the Erector Set components used to build the animated scenes. Erector parts can be ordered via mail using Table 3 as your guide. However, you should always call ahead for prices and availability. As noted in Table 1, Erector Set components may also be seen in person, but only by appointment.

Table 1 Material Source Addresses

Material Category	Name	Address	Telephone
Electric & Electronic Components	Digi-Key Corporation	701 Brooks Ave. South, P.O.Box 677 Theif River Falls, MN 56701-0677 www.digikey.com	1-800-344-4539
Electric & Electronic Components	Mouser Electronics	958 North Main Street Mansfield, TX 76063-4827 www.mouser.com	1-800-346-6873
Electric & Electronic Components	Radio Shack	Local Area Stores	
Electric & Electronic Components	Tech America	P.O. Box 1981 Fort Worth, TX 76101-1981 www.techam.com	1-800-877-0072
Erector Set Parts	Wagner & Sons Toys & Trains (Walk-in Erector parts by appointment only.)	28 East Willow Street Carlisle, PA 17013 www.wagerandsonstoys.com	717-258-0839 1-800-821-7002
Light Bulbs	Charlie's Trains	P.O. Box 158 Hubertus, WI 53033 FAX 414-628-2651	414-628-1544
Light Bulbs	Town & Country Hobbies & Crafts	26 Dewey Avenue Totowa Boro, NJ 07512	973-942-5176
Motors & Electric Components	Edmund Scientific Company	101 East Gloucester Pike Barrington, NJ 08007-1380 www.edsci.com	1-800-728-6999
Motors & Electric Components	Herbach & Rademan Co.	16 Roland Avenue Mt. Laurel, NJ 08054 www.herbach.com	1-800-848-8001
O Gauge Accessories	Berkshire Valley, Inc.	P.O. Box 150 Adams, MA 01220 www.berkshirevalleyinc.com	1-800-984-0591
O Gauge Figures/Accessories	Arttista Accessories	105 Woodring Lane Newark, DE 19707 www.quikpage.com/A/arttista	302-455-0195 1-800-316-2493
O Gauge Figures/Accessories	Bowser Manufacturing Co.	P.O. Box 322, 21 Howard St. Montoursville , PA 17754 www.bowser-trains.com	717-368-2379

Table 2   Electrical Items

Item	Item No.	Vendor No.	Source
Bridge rectifier, 1.4 Amp, 100 PIV		583-RB152	Mouser Electronics
Bridge rectifier, 1.4 Amp, 100 PIV		276-1152	Radio Shack
Capacitor, .01 μf, 50 VDC		140-PF1H103K	Mouser Electronics
Capacitor, .01 μf, 50 VDC		272-1065	Radio Shack
Capacitor, .047 μf, 50 VDC		140-PF1H473K	Mouser Electronics
Capacitor, .047 μf, 50 VDC		272-1068	Radio Shack
Capacitor, electrolytic, radial leads, 1000 μf, 35 VDC		539-TKR35V1000	Mouser Electronics
Capacitor, electrolytic, radial leads, 1000 μf, 35 VDC		272-1032	Radio Shack
Capacitor, electrolytic, radial leads, 220 μf, 35 VDC		539-TKR50V220	Mouser Electronics
Capacitor, electrolytic, radial leads, 220 μf, 35 VDC		272-1029	Radio Shack
Capacitor, Tantalum, 10 μf, ± 10%, 16 VDC		581-10K16V	Mouser Electronics
Capacitor, Tantalum, 10 μf, ± 20%, 35 VDC		RSU 11295946	Radio Shack
Capacitor, Tantalum, 2.2 μf, ± 10%, 16 VDC		581-2.2K16V	Mouser Electronics
Capacitor, Tantalum, 2.2 μf, ± 20%, 35 VDC		RSU 11295888	Radio Shack
Capacitor, Tantalum, 22 μf, ± 10%, 16 VDC		581-22K16V	Mouser Electronics
Capacitor, Tantalum, 22 μf, ± 20%, 35 VDC		RSU 11295961	Radio Shack
Capacitor, Tantalum, 47 μf, ± 10%, 16 VDC		581-47K16V	Mouser Electronics
Capacitor, Tantalum, 47 μf, ± 20%, 35 VDC		RSU 11295987	Radio Shack
Connector, 2 pin male/female set, polarized, interlocking		274-222	Radio Shack
Connector, 4 pin female, polarized, interlocking		274-234	Radio Shack
Connector, 4 pin male, polarized, interlocking		274-224	Radio Shack
Connector, 6 pin female, polarized, interlocking		274-236	Radio Shack
Connector, 6 pin male, polarized, interlocking		274-226	Radio Shack
Diode, 1N4001, 50 PIV	1N4001	583-1N4001	Mouser Electronics
Diode, 1N4001, 50 PIV	1N4001	276-1101	Radio Shack
Fan, Micro 12VDC, 150 ma.		273-240	Radio Shack
Heat sink for TO-220 case Iintegrated circuit		532-507302B00	Mouser Electronics
Heat sink for TO-220 case integrated circuit		276-1363	Radio Shack
Lamp socket, miniature bayonet base with solder tabs		272-355	Radio Shack
Lamp, 12 volt, grain-of-wheat with 12" leads, clear			Hobby Stores
Lamp, 14 volt, .08 A., midget flange base, clear	330	353-0330	Mouser Electronics
Lamp, 14 volt, .08 A., midget flange base, clear	330	RSU 11673399	Radio Shack
Lamp, 14 volt, .24 A, miniature bayonet, clear	57		Charlie's Trains
Lamp, 14 volt, .24 A, miniature bayonet, clear	57		Town & Country
Lamp, 16 volt, grain-of-wheat with 12" leads, clear			Hobby Stores
Lamp, 18 volt, .15 A, small round, min. bayonet, clear	1445		Charlie's Trains
Lamp, 18 volt, .15 A, small round, min. bayonet, clear	1445		Town & Country
Lamp, 6.3 volt, .25 A, tubular, min.bayonet, clear	44	606-CM44	Mouser Electronics
Lamp, 6.3 volt, .25 A, tubular, min.bayonet, clear	44	272-1108	Radio Shack
Lamp, 7 volt, .41 A, large round, min.bayonet, clear	55		Charlie's Trains
Lamp, 7 volt, .41 A, large round, min.bayonet, clear	55	CM55-ND	Digi-Key Corporation
Lamp, T-1 wire terminal, 5 volt, .06 A., clear	683	CM683-ND	Digi-Key Corporation
Lamp, T-1 wire terminal, 5 volt, .06 A., clear	683	353-0683	Mouser Electronics
LEDs ≈.1" diameter, red		351-3102	Mouser Electronics
Momentary pushbutton, SPST, normally closed		275-1556	Radio Shack
Motor, 1 rpm, 12 VDC, reversible, 1/8" shaft, cont. run		V41-860	Edmund Scientific
Motor, 115 rpm, 12 VDC, reversible, 1/8" shaft, cont. run		V41-867	Edmund Scientific

88

Item	Item No.	Vendor No.	Source
Motor, 16 rpm, 12 VDC, reversible, 1/8" shaft, cont. run		V41-865	Edmund Scientific
Motor, 2 rpm, 12 VDC, reversible, 1/8" shaft, cont. run		V41-331	Edmund Scientific
Motor, 30 rpm, 12 VDC, reversible, 1/8" shaft, cont. run		V41-333	Edmund Scientific
Motor, 7 rpm, 12 VDC, reversible, 1/8" shaft, cont. run		V41-863	Edmund Scientific
Motors, miscellaneous surplus			Herbach & Rademan
PC Board, dual general purpose, predrilled, IC		276-159	Radio Shack
PC Board, multipurpose, predrilled, indexed, IC		276-150	Radio Shack
PC Board, multipurpose, predrilled, indexed, LSI-IC		RSU 10524494	Radio Shack
Project box - approximately: 6" x 3" x 2"		RSU 11907623	Radio Shack
Project box - approximately: 7" x 4" x 2 ½"		RSU 11907714	Radio Shack
Relay, DIP, 12 VDC, 280 ohm coil, DPDT, 1 A contacts		275-249	Radio Shack
Relay, DIP, 12 VDC, 960 ohm coil, DPDT, 1 A contacts		431-OVR-SH-212L	Mouser Electronics
Resistor, 10Ω, ± 5%, 10 watts		28PR009-10	Mouser Electronics
Resistor, 10Ω, ± 5%, 3 watts		28PR004-10	Mouser Electronics
Resistor, 10Ω, ± 5%, 5 watts		900-0921	Tech America
Resistor, 10Ω, 10 watts		271-132	Radio Shack
Resistor, 100Ω, ± 5%, ½ watt		30BJ500-100	Mouser Electronics
Resistor, 100Ω, ± 5%, ½ watt		271-1108	Radio Shack
Resistor, 100KΩ, ± 5%, ½ watt		30BJ500-100K	Mouser Electronics
Resistor, 100KΩ, ± 5%, ½ watt		271-1131	Radio Shack
Resistor, 10KΩ, ± 5%, ½ watt		30BJ500-10K	Mouser Electronics
Resistor, 10KΩ, ± 5%, ½ watt		271-1126	Radio Shack
Resistor, 15Ω, ± 5%, ½ watt		30BJ500-15	Mouser Electronics
Resistor, 15Ω, ± 5%, ½ watt		271-1102	Radio Shack
Resistor, 150Ω, ± 5%, ½ watt		30BJ500-150	Mouser Electronics
Resistor, 150Ω, ± 5%, ½ watt		271-1109	Radio Shack
Resistor, 150Ω, ± 5%, 10 watts		28PR009-150	Mouser Electronics
Resistor, 150Ω, ± 5%, 10 watts		900-1077	Tech America
Resistor, 150KΩ, ± 5%, ¼ watt		RSU 11345287	Radio Shack
Resistor, 150KΩ, ± 5%, ½ watt		30BJ500-150K	Mouser Electronics
Resistor, 1MΩ, ± 5%, ½ watt		30BJ500-1M	Mouser Electronics
Resistor, 1MΩ, ± 5%, ½ watt		271-1134	Radio Shack
Resistor, 2.2MΩ, ± 5%, ½ watt		30BJ500-2.2M	Mouser Electronics
Resistor, 2.2MΩ, ± 5%, ½ watt		271-1135	Radio Shack
Resistor, 22Ω, ± 5%, ½ watt		30BJ500-22	Mouser Electronics
Resistor, 22Ω, ± 5%, ½ watt		271-1103	Radio Shack
Resistor, 220KΩ, ± 5%, ½ watt		30BJ500-220K	Mouser Electronics
Resistor, 220KΩ, ± 5%, ½ watt		271-1132	Radio Shack
Resistor, 3Ω, ± 5%, 10 watts		28PR009-3	Mouser Electronics
Resistor, 3Ω, ± 5%, 10 watts		900-1036	Tech America
Resistor, 33Ω, ± 5%, ½ watt		30BJ500-33	Mouser Electronics
Resistor, 33Ω, ± 5%, ½ watt		271-1104	Radio Shack
Resistor, 330KΩ, ± 5%, ¼ watt		RSU 11345352	Radio Shack
Resistor, 330KΩ, ± 5%, ½ watt		30BJ500-330K	Mouser Electronics
Resistor, 33KΩ, ± 5%, ½ watt		30BJ500-33K	Mouser Electronics
Resistor, 33KΩ, ± 5%, ½ watt		271-1129	Radio Shack
Resistor, 390KΩ, ± 5%, ¼ watt		RSU 11345360	Radio Shack
Resistor, 390KΩ, ± 5%, ½ watt		30BJ500-390K	Mouser Electronics

Item	Item No.	Vendor No.	Source
Resistor, 40Ω, ± 5%, 5 watts		28PR004-40	Mouser Electronics
Resistor, 40Ω, ± 5%, 5 watts		900-0935	Tech America
Resistor, 470KΩ, ± 5%, ½ watt		30BJ500-470K	Mouser Electronics
Resistor, 470KΩ, ± 5%, ½ watt		271-1133	Radio Shack
Resistor, 47KΩ, ± 5%, ½ wat		30BJ500-47K	Mouser Electronics
Resistor, 47KΩ, ± 5%, ½ watt		271-1130	Radio Shack
Resistor, 5Ω, ± 5%,10 watts		28PR009-5	Mouser Electronics
Resistor, 5Ω, ± 5%,10 watts		900-1043	Tech America
Resistor, 5.6KΩ, ± 5%, ½ watt		30BJ500-5.6K	Mouser Electronics
Resistor, 5.6KΩ, ± 5%, ½ watt		271-1125	Radio Shack
Resistor, 6.8Ω, ± 5%,10 watts		28PR009-6.8	Mouser Electronics
Resistor, 6.8Ω, ± 5%,10 watts		900-1045	Tech America
Resistor, 6.8KΩ, ± 5%, ½ watt		30BJ500-6.8K	Mouser Electronics
Resistor, 6.8KΩ, ± 5%, ½ watt		900-0399	Tech America
Resistor, 680KΩ, ± 5%, ½ watt		30BJ500-680K	Mouser Electronics
Resistor, 68KΩ, ± 5%, ¼ watt		RSU 11345212	Radio Shack
Resistor, 68KΩ, ± 5%, ½ watt		30BJ500-68K	Mouser Electronics
Resistor, 68KΩ, ± 5%, ½ watt		900-0423	Tech America
Resistor, 8.2Ω, ± 5%, 10 watts		28PR009-8.2	Mouser Electronics
Resistor, 8.2Ω, ± 5%, 10 watts		900-1047	Tech America
Resistor, 8.2KΩ, ± 5%, ½ watt		30BJ500-8.2K	Mouser Electronics
Resistor, 8.2KΩ, ± 5%, ½ watt		900-0401	Tech America
Resistor, 820KΩ, ± 5%, ½ watt		30BJ500-820K	Mouser Electronics
Resistor, 82KΩ, ± 5%, ¼ watt		RSU 11345238	Radio Shack
Resistor, 82KΩ, ± 5%, ½ watt		30BJ500-82K	Mouser Electronics
Resistor, 82KΩ, ± 5%, ½ watt		900-0425	Tech America
Resistor, wirewound, 2Ω, ± 5%,10 watts		28PR009-2	Mouser Electronics
Resistor, wirewound, 2Ω, 10 watts		271-080	Radio Shack
Silicone heat sink grease		524-8109-S	Mouser Electronics
Silicone heat sink grease		276-1373	Radio Shack
Single timer, linear integrated circuit, DIP-8 package	555	511-NE555N	Mouser Electronics
Single timer, linear integrated circuit, DIP-8 package	555	276-1723 (LM555)	Radio Shack
Socket, integrated circuit, 16 pin, DIP		575-199316	Mouser Electronics
Socket, integrated circuit, 16 pin, DIP		276-1998	Radio Shack
Socket, integrated circuit, 8 pin, DIP		575-199308	Mouser Electronics
Socket, integrated circuit, 8 pin, DIP		276-1995	Radio Shack
Speaker, 4" wide range, 2 watts or greater		40-1197	Radio Shack
Toggle switch, SPST, 3 Amp @ 125 VAC		275-602	Radio Shack
Tubing, Flexible Polyolefin, Heat Shrink, 1/8"		517-301018BK	Mouser Electronics
Tubing, Flexible Polyolefin, Heat Shrink, 3/64"		517-301364BK	Mouser Electronics
Voltage regulator, fixed, +12 Volt DC, TO-220 package	7812	511-L7812CP	Mouser Electronics
Voltage regulator, fixed, +12 Volt DC, TO-220 package	7812	276-1771	Radio Shack
Voltage regulator, fixed, +5 Volt DC, TO-220 package	7805	511-L7805CP	Mouser Electronics
Voltage regulator, fixed, +5 Volt DC, TO-220 package	7805	276-1770	Radio Shack
Wire – Bus #24, pretinned, solid		278-1341	Radio Shack

Table 3   Erector Set Components

(Drawings are not to scale.)

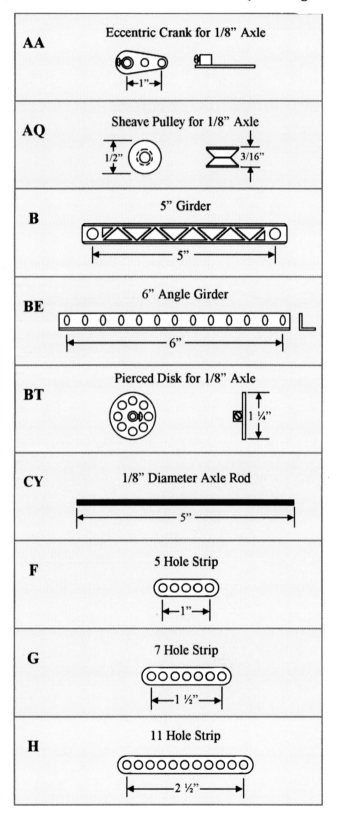

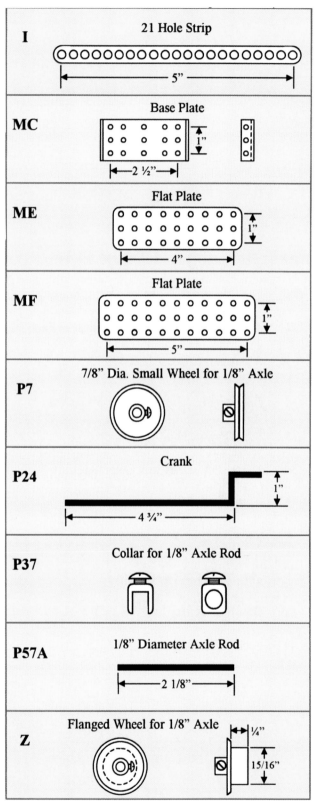

Chapter Nine

Bibliography

No.	Title	Author	Publication	Publication Date
1	Log Cars for Your Layout	Roy Everett	OGR Run 129	June 1993
2	A Visit to the Buena Vista Amusement Park	Roy Everett	OGR Run 136	August 1994
3	A Day at the (Buena Vista) Amusement Park	Not Applicable	OGR, The Video Vol. 1, No. 4	Summer 1994 (July 1994)
4	Operating Lanterns to Light Up Your Pike	Roy Everett	OGR Run 137	October 1994
5	Track Powered Log Car Lanterns	Roy Everett	OGR Run 138	December 1994
6	The SAGA of the Little Lakes Lines	Roy Everett	OGR Run 140	April 1995
7	Realistic Lighting for Your Lionel RC Switches	Roy Everett	OGR Run 142	August 1995
8	Roy Everett's Little Lakes Lines	Not Applicable	OGR, The Video Vol. 2, No. 2	Winter 1995 (January 1996)
9	The "April Fool" Locomotive	Roy Everett	OGR Run 146	April 1996
10	"Hot Box" Reefer	Roy Everett	OGR Run 155	October 1997
11	Flicker-Free Passenger Car Lights	Roy Everett	OGR Run 157	August 1998